The
Women'sHealth
Big Book *of*
Smoothies
& Soups

The Women'sHealth

Big Book of Smoothies & Soups

More than **100** BLENDED RECIPES FOR BOOSTED ENERGY, BRIGHTER SKIN & BETTER HEALTH

The Editors of Women'sHealth

WITH **LISA DeFAZIO**, MS, RD

RODALE

This book is intended as a reference volume only, not as a medical manual. The information given here is designed to help you make informed decisions about your health. It is not intended as a substitute for any treatment that may have been prescribed by your doctor. If you suspect that you have a medical problem, we urge you to seek competent medical help.

Mention of specific companies, organizations, or authorities in this book does not imply endorsement by the author or publisher, nor does mention of specific companies, organizations, or authorities imply that they endorse this book, its author, or the publisher.

Internet addresses and telephone numbers given in this book were accurate at the time it went to press.

© 2016 by Rodale Inc.

All rights reserved. No part of this publication may be reproduced or transmitted in any form or by any means, electronic or mechanical, including photocopying, recording, or any other information storage and retrieval system, without the written permission of the publisher.

Rodale books may be purchased for business or promotional use or for special sales. For information, please write to: Special Markets Department, Rodale Inc., 733 Third Avenue, New York, NY 10017

Women's Health is a registered trademark of Rodale Inc.

Printed in the United States of America

Rodale Inc. makes every effort to use acid-free ∞, recycled paper ♻.

Photo on page xvi, courtesy of Vitamix; page xvii (left), courtesy SharkNinja; page xvii (right), courtesy Hamilton Beach; page 10, Lisa Shin; page 36, Thomas MacDonald/Rodale Images; page 90, iStockPhoto; page 116, Photo Alto; page 144, Rodale Images; page 170, Lisovskaya/Getty Images; page 194, Funkystock/Getty Images; page 248, Corbis Images. All other photos by Mitch Mandel/Rodale Images.

Brown background, first occurrence page ii, Wdstock/Getty Images; white background, first occurrence page vi, Sally Williams/Getty Images; blue background, first occurrence page viii, Mitch Mandel/Rodale Images; border art, first occurrence page 3, DigitalVision Vectors/Getty Images.

Book design by Carol Angstadt

Prop styling by Carla Gonzalez-Hart

Food styling by Diane Vezza

Library of Congress Cataloging-in-Publication Data is on file with the publisher.

ISBN 978-1-62336-787-9

Distributed to the trade by Macmillan

2 4 6 8 10 9 7 5 3 1 paperback

This book is dedicated to my parents,
Dr. and Mrs. Frank and Linda DeFazio.

Contents

ACKNOWLEDGMENTS

I have to thank my agent, Blair Taylor, and my manager, Casandra Franceschi, for taking a chance on me. Blair, your guidance has been invaluable, and you are a role model for what an agent should be. You always put my best interests first, and I am honored to have you represent me. Casandra, thank you for being there for me whenever I need you. Your expertise and honesty have contributed to my success, and I know how fortunate I am to have you as my manager. I look forward to making my career goals happen with you by my side.

Dad, you always pushed me to my fullest potential and told me, "Someday you will do great things." Thank you for guiding me throughout my career and reminding me to never accept less than my worth. Mom, you taught me how to run a household, cook, host dinner parties, and be a strong woman who can handle anything. Thank you for your sacrifices throughout my life and for showing me what a mother should be. I love you both and hope I have made you proud.

This book would not have been possible without the support of my husband. Roy, you encouraged me while I chased my dream of becoming a television and media nutritionist. Thank you for giving me the opportunity to leave a full-time job to achieve my ultimate career goal. This is just the beginning—I love you! Last but not least, I dedicate this book to my son, Nicolas. You are my angel, and I am so grateful to be your mother. Thank you for your patience while I wrote this book. You have taught me what really matters in life. I am so proud of you and I love you.

—Lisa

INTRODUCTION

When it comes to great health, there's one thing the editors at *Women's Health* and I know for sure: Eating more whole fruits and veggies is transformative for your body. We also know it's not always easy to eat healthy. There are temptations surrounding us, especially quick-and-easy convenience foods. Our solution? Make healthy meals fast and delicious. So we teamed up to provide you with a range of soups and smoothies that you can make easily and enjoy no matter what time of day or year.

But this is not your typical recipe book. It's really three books in one: a cookbook, nutrition guide, and health-troubleshooting handbook. Every recipe has been carefully created with a purpose. Each chapter addresses a specific health issue, and the ingredients used in each recipe were chosen specifically to treat that issue. Have a cold? Try a soup with garlic. Menstrual cramps? A smoothie with banana should do the trick. We've got your every health concern covered.

Soups and smoothies are an easy way to pack a ton of fruits and vegetables into your diet. We all know we need to eat more of them, but after reading this book you will realize *why* they are so critical for your health and exactly *how* the nutrients in these foods help your body. In my 20 years of practice as a registered dietitian and nutritionist, I have found that when people understand *why* they should eat or avoid certain foods, they are more excited and motivated to follow my advice on their path to better health.

WHY SOUPS & SMOOTHIES?

Some may argue that eating the fruits and vegetables whole would be better than blending them. That may be true in a perfect world, but this is not a perfect world. Let's be honest: Very few of us get the recommended daily amounts of fruits, vegetables, vitamins, and minerals we're supposed to. We are so busy with work and family responsibilities that getting a healthy meal prepared is just not going to happen at every breakfast, lunch, and dinner of the week. That is where this book will *save* you. Smoothies and soups are a great way to embrace life's chaos without compromising your health (and sanity). Blending foods retains all of the good stuff—the fiber, vitamins, minerals, and other nutrients. The fiber fills you up and aids digestion. In contrast, juicing throws out the fiber and leaves you with a drink that can be high in sugar.

The soup recipes ahead are designed to make 4 servings. They're super easy to prepare and simmer on the stove while you're home relaxing, binge-watching Netflix, or doing laundry. And soup isn't just for the chilly winter months. We've included recipes that are perfect for summertime sipping as well! When it comes to storage, refrigerate the soup in food storage containers or mason jars. If you want to freeze it, keep in mind that liquids expand while freezing and plastic containers often have harmful chemicals, so be sure to use glass containers and do not fill the container to the top. Leave about an inch between the soup and the lid to allow for expansion. That way you can quickly heat up the soup and serve it on the go.

Soup is your best friend on a hectic day. It's the perfect afternoon snack to hold you over until dinner, and it also helps control calorie intake. According to a study at Pennsylvania State University, eating low-calorie soup before a meal can reduce the number of calories you consume during the meal. The participants in the study who had soup before their entree reduced their total calorie intake by 20 percent compared to those who did not have soup. It might not sound huge, but anything that helps curb overeating really makes a difference in your overall health, whether you're trying to slim down or just stay satisfied with real, nutritious foods.

We also love smoothies—who doesn't? Smoothies are ideal for breakfast, especially on days when you have to get out of the house early. They're super easy to blend and enjoy while you're on the go.

We've combined the healthiest ingredients to flush your body with nutrients. That includes some veggies too! But don't be afraid. Bright green smoothies with kale or spinach may look unappetizing, but we promise, we've carefully chosen ingredient combinations so that you won't even taste the vegetables. Most of the smoothies also contain protein from nut butters or yogurt, so these can be used as meal replacements that will keep you energized throughout the morning and all day long.

BACK TO BASICS: WHOLE FOODS

There's a reason the Standard American Diet acronym is SAD. In 2016, the typical American diet was loaded with processed foods. The scariest part is that you may not even know you're consuming them! To clean up your health, you simply must eat more real, whole foods, aka "clean" foods. So what are "whole foods"? Whole foods are foods in their natural state, with all of the vitamins, minerals, and other nutrients. Whole foods are not refined or processed in a factory. They go from the ground or tree or farm right to your table.

Processed foods are bad for us because they're made in factories that strip whole foods of nutrients and add sugar, salt, and other ingredients to enhance flavor, texture, and color. Sadly, processed foods have become the foundation of the American diet, and that is partly why obesity rates are so high. Many Americans survive on fast food, snack foods, and soda, but the body can only take so much fat, sugar, and salt. Over time, diabetes, high blood pressure, weight gain, and other major health issues develop. That's why we want to help you get back to basics: whole foods that provide your body with the fuel it needs to function properly and stay healthy.

Although we emphasize whole foods, we did include some packaged foods in the recipes. But don't worry, they are still good for you and make life a little easier. Ingredients like low-sodium broth, coconut milk (in a carton, not canned!), almond milk, peanut butter, and canned beans were selected because they save time but are still healthy. If you prefer making your own peanut butter, coconut milk, and broth from scratch, go for it!

NUTRITION COMES FIRST

I have been a registered dietitian and nutritionist for the past 20 years. I've worked as a health educator, teaching classes on everything from weight loss and diabetes to heart disease and how to quit smoking. I've taught and counseled thousands of patients to lose weight and manage their medical issues with diet and lifestyle changes. I truly turned my passion into my profession, and I love educating and supporting people as they take control of their health.

I really believe I was *destined* to be a nutritionist. Throughout high school and college, I worked at a nearby health club, checking in members at the front desk and teaching them how to use the various exercise machines and weights. The gym became a big part of my life. I would exercise there after work and socialize with my coworkers. My daily routine throughout high school and college was working out, working, attending college, and studying. I have always been disciplined, and I knew that if I had a successful career, I would be able to live the life I wanted in the future. This was my daily motivation to study and prioritize what was important. I was never a "party girl" in college and I did not drink that much or experiment with drugs. (I've never even smoked a cigarette!)

Needless to say, health is my passion—but I realize everyone is on a different point on his or her wellness journey. Maybe you're just beginning to take an interest in your health, or maybe you're looking for even more healthy ideas. It doesn't matter where you are, as long as you have a desire to nourish yourself and feel better. I've seen patients of all shapes and sizes become healthier, starting with their diet. This book will get you there.

WOMEN'S HEALTH

If you're a reader of *Women's Health*, then you already know that the editors are obsessed with helping women reach their fitness, weight loss, and nutrition goals. Each month, the editors scour every health study and medical journal, interviewing the country's leading experts for the most up-to-date information on how to help women take charge of their bodies and minds. *Women's Health* makes it a priority to deliver authoritative, evidence-based advice so you're never left in the dark on any health issue, diet fad, or exercise plan, and now we've teamed up to give you our take on soups and smoothies. Together, we promise to help bring new vibrancy to your life through healthful blended meals. We're not interested in short-term gimmicks that don't last. We're here to transform your lifestyle for the long run. Soups and smoothies are loaded with the best nutrients to keep you glowing inside and out. You're going to look and feel great! Consider it our unbreakable promise.

READY? SET? BLEND!

Now that you know the basics of real, whole foods, soups, and smoothies, you're ready to get started! Not sure where to begin? You could pinpoint a problem, from low energy to menstrual cramps, and start with a soup or smoothie designed to alleviate those symptoms. Or maybe there's a particular ingredient you're craving. Check out the Index for a soup or smoothie ingredient that strikes your fancy. We'll be there along the way with tips, tricks, and even some fun DIY projects. Now grab your blender, fruits, and veggies, and dive into better health!

BUYING THE RIGHT BLENDER

The genius of soups and smoothies is that you don't need a lot of kitchen experience or equipment. But obviously, there's one tool you can't do without: a blender. You'll find them at all price points, with lots of different features. We explain below, but remember that whether you're able to splurge on a Vitamix or need to dig out the drugstore version your mom bought you in college, the most important thing is to start using it!

VITAMIX PROFESSIONAL SERIES 750 BLACK WITH 64-OUNCE CONTAINER ($600)

If you are looking for the best blender you can buy and you are not on a budget, the Vitamix 750 is for you. Here are some of its features.

• Manual speed control: A manual control lets you slowly increase the blender's speed, which prevents the "tornado effect" that makes it tricky to blend smoothies evenly. When a blender goes immediately to high speed, it makes air bubbles inside the pitcher, preventing the liquids and frozen ingredients from mixing, which creates chunky smoothies.

• Large plastic pitcher: The 8-cup pitcher is helpful when adding frozen ingredients, as they can be large, and when blending large batches of soup.

• Tamper: This is a tool that helps to blend thick, dense ingredients. It is used to push food down into the Vitamix processing blades but does not come into contact with the blades.

• Multipronged blades: If you will be adding ice, frozen fruit, and other hard ingredients, you'll want multipronged blades to crush and liquefy them.

NINJA PROFESSIONAL BLENDER ($110)

If you want a quality blender for a reasonable price, then the Ninja Professional Blender is a great option! Features include:

- **A powerful motor:** The 1,000-watt motor is just about as powerful as those in some of the more expensive blenders.

- **Sharp, unique blades:** A unique stacked blade design helps this blender perform. The blade extends the length of the blender. It consists of three pairs of blades, staggered along a long stem. This design blends ingredients evenly.

- **Large plastic 72-ounce pitcher with a pouring spout:** This is great for blending big batches of soups or a few smoothie servings at one time.

- **Performance:** The Ninja Professional really keeps up with blenders that are four or five times its price, blending ice and frozen fruit easily.

HAMILTON BEACH WAVE CRUSHER MULTIFUNCTION BLENDER ($40)

For a very affordable blender that will do the job on a budget, this is a fantastic choice. Check out its qualities.

- **Performance:** The blender is very powerful and can puree, liquefy, blend, mix, chop, and crush ice.

- **Good-size glass pitcher:** The 40-ounce glass pitcher has a pour lid with a spout and dishwasher-safe parts.

- **Unique function:** The wave-action system forces foods and liquids down into the blades for a smoother result.

- **Variety of functions:** Settings include dice, stir, milkshake, chop, puree, smoothie, grind, crush ice, easy clean, mix, salsa, whip, grate, and icy drink.

Aging in Reverse

Turn Back the Clock

Let's face it—life is busy! And sometimes it wears on us. Stress, alcohol, sun exposure, and poor eating habits can take a toll—especially on our skin. While we all want the wisdom that comes with age, we don't want the wrinkles, dull skin, or dark circles! Sure, you could slather on face creams and serums, subject yourself to harsh peels and microdermabrasion, even rub an avocado-honey-oatmeal-yogurt mask on your face, but the truth is that what you eat is the best beauty regimen around. You can't actually turn back time, as Cher wistfully sang, but you *can* nourish yourself with smart, simple blended smoothies and soups that pack a powerful antiaging punch.

ANTIAGING 101

Why does our skin start to sag, crease, and darken over time? Free radicals, which come from metabolic processes in our bodies or from outside sources such as stress, lack of sleep, fried foods, alcohol, air pollution, sun exposure (UV rays), x-rays, cigarette smoking, and pesticides, damage our skin cells and tissues and cause oxidation. Oxidation is when free radicals break down a cell's components, such as its proteins, DNA, and membranes. When oxidation occurs, cells lose their ability to function properly. Think of how a sliced apple starts to turn brown. Yup. Free radical damage causes skin wrinkles, lines, dehydration, sagging, and loss of youthful volume. Free radicals also cause inflammation, which is not limited to the damaged areas but can also spread to healthy tissue, destroying collagen and elastin and leading to additional premature sagging, fine lines, and wrinkles.

This may sound depressing and inevitable, but there's hope! Antioxidants have the ability to counteract the effects of free radicals and slow down the aging process. Your body can manufacture some antioxidants, but its ability to produce them declines as you age. Therefore, it's important to pack your diet with antiaging superstar antioxidants like vitamins A, C, and E to protect your skin from damage. In addition, these beauty boosters increase collagen production, repair elasticity, reduce UV damage, alleviate inflammation, reduce breakouts, and enhance texture of skin.

SAVOR YOUR WAY TO BETTER SKIN

Everything you eat and drink contributes to the way you look, and the best news is that eating your way to a youthful glow has never been easier or more delicious! Start by nourishing your body with antiaging superstars like berries, cucumber, watermelon, and tomatoes, and you'll quickly look and feel healthy, happy, and more vibrant—from the inside out.

We're always being told to drink more water, but do you *really* know why? Our body's cells, organs, and tissues need to be hydrated in order to function. Water has an incredible number of roles: It controls temperature, removes wastes, lubricates joints, and transports nutri-

ANTIAGING SUPERSTARS

- **Berries of all colors are antioxidant rich, which means they fight free radicals, molecules that cause cell damage and are linked to chronic inflammation.**

- **Spinach and dark leafy greens contain lutein and zeaxanthin, plant pigments that protect your eyes from the harmful effects of ultraviolet light.**

- **Cucumbers have the highest water content of any solid food and keep your skin hydrated and happy.**

- **Sweet potatoes are high in beta-carotene, which converts to vitamin A and restores skin elasticity, promotes skin cell turnover, and maintains soft, youthful skin.**

- **Carrots are also high in beta-carotene and likewise restore skin elasticity, promote skin cell turnover, and keep skin bright.**

- **Citrus fruits contain vitamin C, which fights wrinkles and aids in the production of collagen, the structural protein in skin.**

- **Watermelon is 92 percent water—that's a lot of skin hydration!**

- **Tomatoes are rich in lycopene, which keeps your skin firm as it reduces the activity of enzymes that break down collagen.**

- **Pomegranates help your skin stay healthy by boosting collagen production, keeping your skin firm and wrinkle free.**

- **Turmeric repairs sun-damaged skin and prevents unwanted wrinkles.**

ents. The balance between electrolytes and water also determines how well other organ systems function. So, contrary to what you might think, water is not just important for hydration.

Dehydration, which can be caused simply by a hard, sweaty workout, can lead to a host of issues including dizziness, fainting, fever, heart palpitations, decreased urination, increased heart rate, decreased blood pressure, and a swollen tongue. (*Note:* If you are experiencing these signs, cool off any way you can and begin to slowly increase your water intake.)

Another unfortunate manifestation of inadequate water intake is dry, wrinkled skin. As we age, our bodies' tissues cannot retain water as well as they did when we were younger, thus our skin loses the ability to repair itself. But by drinking at least eight 12-ounce glasses of water daily, you will hydrate your body and lessen the appearance of dry, wrinkled skin.

If you find it hard to remember to guzzle water all day, try keeping a reusable water bottle on hand (try glass or stainless steel to avoid the damaging chemicals in plastic bottles). You can also add a couple slices of lemon, lime, or cucumber to give your water a healthy kick. There are even flavor-infusing water bottles that allow you to add fruit and other ingredients for a twist on your hydration. *Pro tip:* Set a reminder on your phone or computer to drink up!

Good Fat Is Your BFF

You may have heard that fat isn't the diet enemy that it was when leg warmers were still in style. Yup, it's time: Our bodies—and especially our skin—need a certain amount of healthy fats to thrive. So what is "good" fat? "Good" fats are monounsaturated, such as olive oil, and polyunsaturated, such as omega-3 fatty

acids. They keep our skin soft and transport vitamins. Omega-3s are found in fatty fish (salmon, trout, catfish, mackerel) as well as flaxseeds and walnuts. Monounsaturated fats are liquid at room temperature but become solid when refrigerated. These fats contain vitamin E. Excellent sources of monounsaturated fats include olives, avocados, hazelnuts, almonds, Brazil nuts, cashews, sesame seeds, pumpkin seeds, and olive, canola, and peanut oils.

"Bad" fats, on the other hand, clog arteries and are not heart friendly. Saturated fats and trans fats are mainly found in dairy and meat products. Trans fats lower your HDL (good cholesterol), elevate your LDL (bad cholesterol), and increase your chances of having diabetes, strokes, and heart disease. Uh, no thanks! Artificial trans fats are the most damaging—these are processed when liquid vegetable oils are heated and combined with hydrogen gas (a process called hydrogenation). Partially hydrogenating vegetable oils preserves them, which is good for food manufacturers, but not good for you!

Although the FDA suggests that you

limit trans fat intake to no more than 2 grams per day, many others in health care recommend that your daily intake should be zero. Examples of bad fats include those found in packaged snacks, most fried foods, commercially baked goods, premixed products, and anything with "partially hydrogenated oil" listed on the food label. Our advice? Stick to fresh, whole foods, nuts and seeds, and, as much as possible, avoid anything with weird-sounding ingredients you can't pronounce.

EAT FOR BETTER EYESIGHT

Okay, maybe you're not ready for bifocals yet, but thanks to Smartphones and ODing on screen time, we strain our eyes more than ever. Cutting back on screen time and wearing sun-protective lenses help, but your diet can, too.

Of course, it'll help your peepers to take a break from all that screen time. A 2015 report from the Vision Council found that 61 percent of Americans have experienced eye strain after prolonged use of electronic devices. Part of the problem is that we tend to open our eyelids wider and blink less frequently when we're staring at screens, and fatigue kicks in because we're focusing on a screen at a fixed distance for a prolonged period without looking away. Many health care providers recommend the "20-20-20 Rule," which means every 20 minutes, take a 20-second break and look off into the distance at something about 20 feet away. This relaxes your eyes and stimulates blinking to remoisten the surface of the eyes—all comforting things!

In addition, you might splurge on a pair of UVA/UVB-blocking shades. And you can actually add certain foods to your diet in order to maintain healthy eyesight. Lutein, beta-carotene, copper, zinc, and vitamins A, C, and E are crucial ingredients that can help protect the surface of your cornea and reduce the risks of cataracts and macular degeneration. A study in the *American Journal of Clinical Nutrition* found that diets higher in lutein and zeaxanthin, a type of carotenoid that decreases the risk of certain cancers and eye diseases, resulted in improvements in patients with age-related macular degeneration. And a study in the *Archives of Ophthalmology* also found that participants who ate the most foods containing lutein and zeaxanthin had a 35 percent lower risk of developing age-related macular degeneration than those who ate the least.

Okay, so what does this all mean?

Your eyes are craving foods like kale, spinach, broccoli, zucchini, Brussels sprouts, and peas, all of which contain lutein and zeaxanthin. If you're not obsessed with kale, don't worry: The recipes in this chapter blend veggies effortlessly into tropical smoothies and creamy soups so yummy you won't even notice the greens.

STRESS LESS

Yeah, we all know stress is the number one thing (besides time) that can age you. And getting me-time is great—if you can manage it. But since most of us can't find time to breathe normally, let alone deeply while meditating for an hour each day, try this technique: Eat the stress away. Now that can be a bad thing if you approach it the wrong way (read: burger, fries, and shake three times a week), but when you're making delicious soups and smoothies using naturally stress-melting ingredients, we can't think of a more enjoyable way to lower our cortisol levels.

These recipes are so easy to prepare, you'll have at *least* 30 seconds to stop, close your eyes, and take a few deep, cleansing breaths before mixing them up. Practicing relaxation techniques like deep breathing, yoga, or meditation is key to reducing your overall stress. If you haven't tried it, you're missing out. But don't just take it from us! A study at the University of North Carolina at Charlotte found that meditation-trained participants showed a significant improvement in their critical cognitive skills—and performed significantly better in cognitive tests than a control group—after only 4 days of training for only 20 minutes each day. Try to find even 10 minutes a day to sit or lie down quietly, close your eyes, and release all your thoughts and worries. You'll be surprised how much more energy you'll have afterward!

And if you have a little more time, feel free to go beyond just 10 minutes of relaxation. Remember to schedule some for yourself, whether that's for a mani-pedi, facial, girls' night out, or long-over-due jog in the park. You can even try setting daily, weekly, and monthly positive affirmations for yourself. For example, you can write down affirmations in a notebook or even in your phone. Do the things that make you happy and ease off on the tendency to self-criticize. You will look and feel younger when you start taking care of *you*!

Fun facts about ...
TURMERIC

Most Powerful Spice on the Planet?

Turmeric is arguably one of the healthiest spices in existence. That's because it has been shown to fight and reverse diseases including inflammation, high cholesterol, and depression. Right now, more than 6,000 peer-reviewed articles have been published about the benefits of turmeric and its compound curcumin.

Here's the best part: Ground turmeric adds a tasty kick to foods and costs just a few dollars per jar. It's been compared to mustard and relish, with hints of orange and ginger. You can use it to replace saffron, which is often more expensive. If turmeric isn't your favorite flavor, no problem. You can add a little to almost anything to receive its fantastic benefits without even noticing its strong taste. We like to put just a pinch in soups *and* smoothies. For a quick, healthy meal, check out the recipe for Spicy Sweet Potato Soup on page 26.

SOOTHE YOUR BELLY

Tummy in knots? Turmeric is great for quelling an upset stomach. That's because it helps with indigestion, ulcers, and gas.

According to the National Institutes of Health, consuming 500 milligrams four times a day can treat a stomachache.

BEAT INFLAMMATION

You're probably familiar with what inflammation looks like when you sprain an ankle—that swollen red area is the result of cells rushing to help repair an injured area. Turns out, the same process happens inside the body, too. Recent research on inflammation has likened it to chronic conditions such as arthritis and fibromyalgia. It can be triggered or exacerbated by poor diet and cause general exhaustion, achiness, and unhappiness. But turmeric has proven anti-inflammatory properties that can help alleviate symptoms.

Health Perk

Did you know that turmeric can also be used to whiten your teeth? It's true! The astringent properties of the spice are believed to keep your teeth pearly and white! Former Miss USA Susie Castillo puts turmeric in her homemade toothpaste. That's great advice from someone who depends on her bright smile.

Live Longer

According to Dr. Andrew Weil, founder and director of the Arizona Center for Integrative Medicine, some of the longest-lived people on the planet, Okinawans, drink copious amounts of turmeric tea. If that's not your, um, cup of tea, try adding ginger and honey for a deliciously zesty, sweet brew.

FIGHT MEMORY LOSS

One of the biggest worries people have today, now that we are living longer, is Alzheimer's disease. While it's unclear exactly what causes Alzheimer's, we know that brain plaque buildup is a big contributor to memory loss, and there are key studies explaining what can prevent or minimize it. In a clinical trial conducted by the *Journal of Neurochemistry*, mice that consumed curcumin extract (found in turmeric) had a 30 percent decrease in brain plaque in 1 week! That's a pretty compelling result considering this is such a mysterious disease.

COOL AS A CUCUMBER SMOOTHIE

MAKES 1 SERVING

You could try to balance slippery cucumber slices on your eyes *or* you could mix up this delicious, hydrating smoothie that fights signs of aging! In addition to fiber-rich cucumber, this smoothie blends in cantaloupe—loaded with vitamins A and C, which promote skin cell turnover and contribute to collagen formation, giving skin elasticity and youthful plumpness. Cucumber and cantaloupe are also high in potassium, which is critical for hydration, as is the coconut water, which adds a tropical kick.

---

1 medium cucumber, peeled, seeded, and chopped*

1 cup coconut water

½ cup chopped cantaloupe

½ cup chopped papaya

1 small lemon, peeled, quartered, and seeded

Several ice cubes

In a blender, combine the cucumber, coconut water, cantaloupe, papaya, lemon, and ice cubes. Blend until the desired consistency is reached. Serve ice cold.

Per serving: 143 calories, 1 g fat (0 g saturated fat), 35 g carbohydrates, 26 g sugar, 69 mg sodium, 5 g fiber, 4 g protein

✳ For best results, chill all ingredients before preparing.

Did you know?

Sodium and potassium are the two primary electrolytes in your body, working together to maintain fluid balance in cells, blood plasma, and extracellular fluid. Along with sodium, potassium regulates the water balance and the acid-base balance in the blood and tissues. Potassium even helps generate muscle contractions and regulate the heartbeat. Eating enough potassium is easy with this satisfying smoothie!

CHERRY REJUVENATOR

MAKES 1 SERVING

This nutrient-dense smoothie promotes total-body regeneration. Cherries contain melatonin, a powerful antioxidant that is critical for healthy sleep. Cherries and nectarines contain high levels of beta-carotene, which, when converted to vitamin A, helps build and maintain healthy skin. And we sneak in some lutein-rich spinach, which helps lower your risk of macular degeneration. Next time you close your eyes, you will know you'll wake up feeling completely refreshed!

1 cup fresh or frozen cherries, pitted*

1 cup spinach

1 nectarine, pitted and sliced, or 1 cup frozen nectarine slices

1 cup unsweetened almond milk or coconut milk

Handful of ice

In a blender, combine the cherries, spinach, nectarine, almond milk or coconut milk, and ice. Blend until the desired consistency is reached. Enjoy!

Per serving: 206 calories, 4 g fat (0 g saturated fat), 43 g carbohydrates, 31 g sugar, 206 mg sodium, 7 g fiber, 5 g protein

✳ A quick way to pit a cherry is to take off the stem and push a drinking straw through the top, twisting gently until the pit pops out the other end.

EYE HEART ORANGE

MAKES 1 SERVING

Blend this bright orange combo to boost your vision as well as your skin. The vitamin A found in carrots and mangoes is critical for eye health, while the vitamin C in mangoes and orange juice protects your skin. Bananas and OJ are loaded with potassium, which helps keep you hydrated.

1 cup orange juice

1 cup sliced carrots

1 small banana

½ cup chopped mango

Handful of ice cubes

In a blender, combine the orange juice, carrots, banana, mango, and ice cubes. Blend until the desired consistency is reached. Enjoy!

Per serving: 303 calories, 1 g fat (0 g saturated fat), 73 g carbohydrates, 50 g sugar, 95 mg sodium, 8 g fiber, 5 g protein

Macular degeneration is the most common cause of vision loss and affects one in four people as they age.

THE BRAZILIAN FACE-LIFT

MAKES 1 SERVING

This powerful skin booster combines kale and blueberries, which are both loaded with antioxidants that help prevent free radical damage and increase collagen production. The secret ingredient here is Brazil nuts—they contain the superstar ingredient selenium (which improves skin's elasticity), plus omega-3 fatty acids and vitamin E (which help to maintain skin's moisture) and copper (which helps melanin production). We'll drink to that!

1 cup coconut water

1 cup chopped kale

1 cup fresh or frozen blueberries

1 orange, peeled

2 Brazil nuts

In a blender, combine the coconut water, kale, blueberries, orange, and Brazil nuts. Blend until the desired consistency is reached. Drink up!

Per serving: 291 calories, 7 g fat (1.5 g saturated fat), 57 g carbohydrates, 37 g sugar, 72 mg sodium, 9 g fiber, 7 g protein

Brazil nuts are the richest in selenium of any food!

ISLAND TIME SHIFTER

This incredibly delicious smoothie is like a tropical Rx for your skin. The mango and strawberries are loaded with vitamins A, C, and E, and avocado is a healthy fat that absorbs vitamins A and E, keeping skin soft and wrinkle free. Almonds add extra fiber and a little crunch for a totally satisfying sip. Frozen fruit is a great way to enjoy out-of-season produce all year long! Bonus: It makes smoothies thick and ice cold (read: extra refreshing and filling).

1 cup fresh or frozen strawberries

1 cup fresh or frozen chopped mango

1 avocado

½ cup unsweetened coconut milk

2 tablespoons shredded unsweetened coconut, divided

10 almonds

1. In a blender, combine the strawberries, mango, avocado, coconut milk, 1 tablespoon of the coconut, and the almonds. Blend until the desired consistency is reached.

2. Sprinkle the remaining 1 tablespoon shredded coconut on top of the smoothie and enjoy!

Per serving: 487 calories, 27 g fat (8 g saturated fat), 65 g carbohydrates, 40 g sugar, 21 mg sodium, 18 g fiber, 8 g protein

TROPICAL TURN-BACK-THE-CLOCK

MAKES 2 SERVINGS

We love a yummy, healthy meal-in-a-bowl, and this one is packed with antioxidant superstar kale, vitamin-rich kiwi, and protein-packed almond butter. Just 1 cup of kale has $3\frac{1}{2}$ times your daily beta-carotene need and loads of vitamin C for glowing skin. Kale also contains alpha-lipoic acid, which helps produce glutathione, which in turn slows the aging process of the eyes, skin, and body.

---

2 frozen bananas

1 cup coconut water or almond milk

1 cup chopped kale

1 kiwifruit, peeled

2 tablespoons almond butter

In a blender, combine the bananas, coconut water or almond milk, kale, kiwi, and almond butter. Blend until the desired consistency is reached. Pour into a bowl. Sprinkle on your toppings and dig in!

Per serving: 707 calories, 31 g fat (9 g saturated fat), 98 g carbohydrates, 46 g sugar, 150 mg sodium, 17 g fiber, 17 g protein

TOPPINGS

2 tablespoons unsweetened shredded coconut

$\frac{1}{4}$ cup pomegranate arils

2 tablespoons chopped almond slices

$\frac{1}{4}$ cup blueberries (or berries of your choice)

Bananas are known as "nature's Botox" because they contain wrinkle-fighting nutrients—including vitamins A, C, and E, zinc, and lectin, which help fade age spots and prevent fine lines and wrinkles from forming.

HYDRATING CHILLED CUCUMBER SOUP

MAKES 4 SERVINGS

The high water content of cucumbers makes this soup a hydrating, cooling wonder, while the protein in yogurt is critical for cell growth, building muscle, and repairing tissue. As you age, you need protein to keep your skin healthy and immune system strong.

5 medium cucumbers, seeded and chopped

1½ cups plain low-fat yogurt

⅓ cup olive oil

¼ cup parsley

¼ cup fresh dill

Juice of 1 lemon

1 clove garlic, minced

12 grape tomatoes, for garnish

1. In a blender, combine the cucumbers, yogurt, oil, parsley, dill, lemon juice, and garlic. Blend until the desired consistency is reached. Pour into a large bowl, cover with plastic wrap, and refrigerate for at least 1 hour.

2. Serve in soup bowls, topped with a few grape tomatoes.

Per serving: 253 calories, 20 g fat (3 g saturated fat), 13 g carbohydrates, 10 g sugar, 72 mg sodium, 2 g fiber, 7 g protein

WRINKLE-FIGHTING WATERMELON-TOMATO GAZPACHO

MAKES 4 SERVINGS

This summery soup blends two key fruits that work together to help keep your skin hydrated and glowing. Watermelon contains vitamin C, which maintains collagen, and the lycopene in tomatoes reduces the activity of enzymes that break down collagen, keeping your skin firm and plump!

2 cups cubed seedless watermelon

2 medium tomatoes, chopped

1 small red onion, chopped

1 tablespoon red wine vinegar

3 tablespoons olive oil, divided

1 ounce crumbled feta cheese, for garnish

1. In a blender, combine the watermelon, tomatoes, onion, vinegar, and 1 tablespoon of the oil. Blend until the desired consistency is reached. You can keep it chunky or continue blending for a smoother gazpacho. Pour the soup into a large pitcher and refrigerate for at least 1 hour.

2. Stir the chilled gazpacho before serving, then pour it into bowls. Top with the feta cheese and drizzle with the remaining 2 tablespoons oil.

Per serving: 71 calories, 4 g fat (0.5 g saturated fat), 10 g carbohydrates, 7 g sugar, 5 mg sodium, 1 g fiber, 1 g protein

YOUTHFUL GLOW
VEGGIE SOUP

MAKES 4 SERVINGS

This easy-to-make soup blends a handful of common veggies that are probably hanging out in your fridge right now! We suggest a healthy mix that's loaded with vitamins C and E and beta-carotene, all of which prevent wrinkles, promote skin cell renewal, and keep your skin hydrated and glowing.

2 tablespoons olive oil

½ cup chopped onion

1 clove garlic, minced

4 cups chopped vegetables (we suggest potato, carrot, asparagus, broccoli, celery, sweet potato, squash, green beans, zucchini, cauliflower— but use what you have!)

4 cups low-sodium vegetable broth

1–2 teaspoons chopped fresh herbs* such as basil, marjoram, or oregano

Salt and ground black pepper

1. In a large stockpot over medium-high heat, heat the oil. Add the onion and garlic and cook, stirring frequently, for 5 minutes, or until the onions are transparent.

2. Add the vegetables and cook, stirring, for 5 to 10 minutes, or until they are slightly browned.

3. Stir in the broth, herbs, and salt and pepper to taste. Bring to a boil. Reduce the heat to low and cover. Simmer for 30 minutes, or until the vegetables are very tender. Remove from the heat and let cool slightly.

4. Working in batches, transfer the soup to a blender and puree until smooth. Serve warm.

Per serving: 156 calories, 7 g fat (1 g saturated fat), 20 g carbohydrates, 5 g sugar, 252 mg sodium, 4 g fiber, 3 g protein

✽ For 1 tablespoon of any fresh herb, you can substitute 1 teaspoon dried.

SUPER TORTILLA SOUP

MAKES 4 SERVINGS

You don't have to wait for Cinco de Mayo to serve up this healthy bean blend! It can be a challenge to consume adequate amounts of protein daily, especially if you don't eat meat, but this vegan-friendly soup uses black beans, which are packed with both protein and antioxidants.

2 cups warm water

1 can (14.5 ounces) diced tomatoes, undrained

½ medium red bell pepper, seeded

1 large carrot

1 avocado, chopped

4 sprigs fresh cilantro + additional chopped cilantro for garnish

1 teaspoon salt

1 teaspoon garlic powder

½ teaspoon onion powder

1 can (15 ounces) corn, drained

1 can (15 ounces) black beans, drained and rinsed

Tortilla chips (look for baked or blue corn style), crushed

1. In a large blender, combine the water, tomatoes, bell pepper, carrot, half of the chopped avocado, the cilantro, salt, garlic powder, and onion powder. Puree until completely smooth. Taste and adjust the seasonings as needed.

2. Add the corn and black beans. Pulse once or twice to blend, but keep the soup chunky.

3. Serve the soup topped with a few crushed tortilla chips, chopped cilantro, and the remaining chopped avocado.

Per serving: 220 calories, 5 g fat (1 g saturated fat), 35 g carbohydrates, 5 g sugar, 940 mg sodium, 9 g fiber, 9 g protein

Did you know?

Lutein deficiency can lead to many problems, including cataracts. Keep your eyes strong by eating bell peppers, which contain lutein and zeaxanthin, and carrots, rich in beta-carotene, which protects against eye diseases including cataracts and age-related macular degeneration.

SPICY SWEET POTATO SOUP

MAKES 4 SERVINGS

This delicious, beautifully hued soup combines sweet potatoes and carrots, two powerhouse veggies packed with beta-carotene, vitamin C, and potassium, which keep skin hydrated and wrinkle free.

2 tablespoons olive oil

1 onion, chopped

½ teaspoon ground cardamom

¼ teaspoon ground turmeric

¼ teaspoon ground cinnamon

Salt and freshly ground
black pepper

2 cups water

1 can (14 ounces) low-sodium
chicken or vegetable broth

2 large sweet potatoes, peeled
and chopped

3 carrots, chopped

1. In a large stockpot over medium-high heat, heat the oil. Cook the onion, stirring frequently, for 5 minutes, or until golden brown. Add the cardamom, turmeric, cinnamon, and salt and pepper to taste. Continue to cook, stirring frequently, for 2 to 3 minutes.

2. Add the water and broth. Next, add the sweet potatoes and carrots.

3. Bring the soup to a boil over high heat, then reduce the heat to medium-low, cover, and simmer for 30 minutes, or until the vegetables are tender. Remove the soup from the heat and let it cool slightly. Puree in small batches until smooth. Serve warm.

Per serving: 163 calories, 8 g fat (1 g saturated fat), 22 g carbohydrates, 6 g sugar, 175 mg sodium, 4 g fiber, 4 g protein

Chapter 2

Skin Health

Glow from the Inside Out

Did you know that your body's largest organ is your skin? Our skin acts as a total-body protective shield, letting in or keeping out everything from nutrients to toxins. Of course, we can't always control what crosses our skin's barrier. For example, spending loads of time outdoors in a warm climate means the potential for sun damage, and living in a city exposes you to extra air pollutants (yuck!). But you *can* take charge of your health and help your skin heal itself by nourishing it properly. Skin issues like psoriasis, acne, and wrinkles are ways that your body expresses its internal needs, and you can treat them nutritionally by packing your diet full of nutrient-rich skin boosters. Grab the ingredients in this chapter and blend your way to beautiful skin—from the inside out!

COLLAGEN: YOUR SECRET WEAPON

When we're young, our body is constantly producing collagen, the fibrous protein that connects skin, bone, tendons, muscles, and cartilage. It's the glue that keeps our skin tight and youthful. Collagen proteins give our bodies strength and structure and contribute to the replacement of dead skin cells. Even though it's the most abundant protein in our bodies, collagen production slows around age 40, and after menopause, it declines even faster.

So much for 40 is the new 30, right?

Fortunately, there are collagen-boosting foods that can combat this drop-off such as kale, avocados, mangoes, spinach, fruits, and nuts. Delicious ways to get these foods into your diet include the Cocoa Glow Skin Smoothie on page 40 and the Saving Face Smoothie Bowl on page 47. By incorporating these skin-loving nutrients into your daily diet and drinking plenty of water, you can help your skin look *years* younger.

AVOID SKIN-DAMAGING NO-NO'S

We've gotta say this up front: There are three major enemies of healthy, glowing skin. We call them the three *S*'s of skin damage: processed sweets, smoking, and sun. This may sound like a broken record, but we urge you to avoid these like the plague! No amount of nutrient-rich superfoods can combat the collagen damage that a sun-worshipping or smoking habit incurs, and while we understand that it's tough to quit, we promise it's worth the effort.

Scale Back on Sweets

Processed sweets may feel like comfort foods, but trust us, they are *not* your

skin's friend. A diet high in sugar makes collagen dry and weak. That means those 3 o'clock cookies or afternoon candy bars should be kicked to the curb. The good news: Eliminating processed sugar from your diet does much more than help your skin. It'll give you more energy too! Once you decide to detox from processed sweets, it takes about 10 days for sugar cravings to end, and until then, you can swap your candy habit for natural sweets like raspberries and orange slices. When a recipe calls for a touch of sweetness, maple syrup can add a little nutrition to your dish! It contains significant levels of essential vitamins and minerals such as manganese, riboflavin, zinc, and potassium. In addition, maple syrup contains antioxidants—54 different polyphenols—many like those found in berries, tea, and flaxseeds.

Kick Those Butts: Myriad Cancers

Smoking is a tough addiction to over-come, but it is one of the easiest ways to age skin prematurely. The chemicals in tobacco damage your skin's collagen and elastin. Nicotine, for example, narrows blood vessels in the outer layers of skin, decreasing the delivery of nutrients and oxygen. In other words, it's doing noth-ing for your complexion, and even more

importantly, it dramatically increases your risk of heart disease and a myriad of cancers. There are many products and programs to help you quit, such as nico-tine gum, nicotine patches, medically supervised smoking cessation programs, and even support groups.

Be Safe in the Sun

Sun exposure is another surefire way of damaging collagen production. We know it's tempting to lie out by the pool or spend all day on the beach, but exposing your skin to ultraviolent rays causes rapid collagen breakdown (not to men-tion that it increases your risk of mela-noma). Remember to wear a hat (there are lots of cute options) and load up on sunscreen (at least 30 SPF) to keep your skin looking youthful long term.

And don't even *think* of going near a tanning bed!

CURE COMMON SKIN AILMENTS

For most skin issues, there's an underlying problem such as poor nutrition or environmental causes. It can be easy to give up and blame your skin problems on age or irreversible damage, but the truth is that you *can* be proactive about having healthier skin.

Wrinkles

Ah, wrinkles, those pesky little reminders that we don't live forever. It's true that our bodies produce less collagen as we age, but there are ways we can prevent wrinkles from developing. For example, sun damage, smoking, and even dehydration speed up wrinkle growth. The key is to stay away from ultraviolent rays, lose the cigarettes, and drink plenty of water—and check out the amazing, antioxidant-packed Gotta Glow Puree on page 52, which combines asparagus, fennel, kale, and spinach. Other wrinkle-fighting foods include tomatoes, berries, green tea, nuts, yogurt, and avocados. Bone broth has recently become a hot nutrition trend.

Our ancestors drank bone broth as a means of using every part of an animal. Simmering the bones and ligaments in water releases beneficial compounds like collagen, proline, glycine, and glutamine. Collagen helps form elastin within the skin and helps you keep a youthful glow.

Acne

For you lucky ones, acne is ancient history. Remember the embarrassment of those teenage breakouts? For others, acne continues into adulthood. Acne is mainly triggered by hormonal imbalances like those caused by PMS and stress, but it can also be a sign of poor nutrition. These factors cause the overproduction of sebum, the natural skin oils that transport dead skin cells to the surface. When sebum rises, pores get clogged and acne forms. No matter what your age, if you're dealing with or trying to prevent a breakout, eat plenty of walnuts, salmon, avocados, and flaxseed oil, which contain omega-3s. Omega-3s help clear up inflammation, a major contributor to acne. Also eat fruits and vegetables high in beta-carotene, such as carrots, cantaloupes, and sweet potatoes. Our bodies convert beta-carotene into vitamin A, a key vitamin that clears up skin and keeps it healthy.

Psoriasis

According to the Mayo Clinic, more than three million people suffer from psoriasis each year. It's the not-so-glamorous skin disorder in which the immune system produces skin cells too quickly. Typically, our skin regenerates every 21 to 28 days, but for people with psoriasis it can take only 2 to 6, causing a rash. Triggers include infections, stress, and even common colds. Psoriasis is an inflammatory disease; therefore, following an anti-inflammatory diet can be a huge help in preventing and treating this stubborn condition. Anti-inflammatory foods such as flaxseeds, olive oil, pumpkin seeds, and walnuts are excellent sources of omega-3 fatty acids.

Dry Skin

Feeling dried out? A common misconception is that skin needs oils or lotions to feel smooth and hydrated. In reality, the biggest reason you might experience dry skin is that you're dehydrated, so make sure to fill up on water throughout the day. Your environment (cold weather, winter winds) or day-to-day habits (taking too-hot showers) could also be drying out your skin. To prevent this, make your shower water a little cooler. Also, be sure you're eating plenty of omega-3s, which help your skin lock in moisture. Flaxseed is an excellent source of omega-3s and can be added to virtually any soup or smoothie.

Fun facts about ...
FLAXSEEDS

A Time-Tested Superfood

These days, flaxseeds are everywhere! You can't turn around in a supermarket without seeing them. But flaxseeds have been harvested long before we deemed them a superfood. Starting about 6,000 years ago in the Mediterranean and India, flax has been used for a variety of purposes, including making paper, linen, and linseed oil for paints and varnishes.

Flax is also an incredible food source. Though each seed is smaller than a grain of rice, flax packs a nutritional punch. These seeds are fiber rich and loaded with omega-3s, which detoxifies the body and promotes healthy skin and hair. They're also virtually tasteless, which means you can add them to any soup or smoothie to receive their fantastic benefits.

Flaxseeds grow on a beautiful five-petaled purple flower. The plant can get up to 47 inches high and tolerates many soils and climates throughout the world, including those in China, Russia, Canada, and most regions of the United States. That means you can probably grow it right in your backyard.

FLAX: WHOLE VS. GROUND

Whole flaxseeds have a tough exterior, making them difficult to digest, and will pass through the digestive system without releasing all of their amazing nutritional benefits. Ground flaxseeds (also called flax meal) are more efficiently absorbed by the body. Store-bought flax meal has a short shelf life, so buy flaxseeds whole and grind them as needed in a coffee or spice grinder. Store them in the refrigerator to maintain freshness.

Health Perk

You don't have to eat flaxseeds to get their benefits—grind 'em, then mix them with essential oil and use as a natural skin moisturizer.

The Tiny Micronutrient

You might have heard lately about the miracle of micronutrients, the water- and fat-soluble vitamins and minerals found in foods like root vegetables, legumes, and, of course, flax! The benefits of consuming micronutrients include healthy skin and more energy, and they can help you stay fuller longer too. Add a pinch of flaxseeds to any of the soups and smoothies in this book—or any meal, for that matter—and you'll feel healthier, happier, and more vibrant.

REDUCE HIGH BLOOD PRESSURE

One in three Americans has high blood pressure, according to the Centers for Disease Control and Prevention. That's about 68 million people! The good news is that, according to the American Heart Association, flax and flaxseed oil can help fight high blood pressure due to flax's alpha-linolenic acid content.

FIGHT DEPRESSION

A study done at the Japanese National Center for Biotechnology Information found that foods rich in omega-3, such as flaxseeds, play a critical role in fighting depression. Flaxseeds help stabilize the function of our central nervous systems, creating a whole slew of benefits, including fewer depressive disorders.

BEAT CHOLESTEROL

Whether we're victims of unfortunate genetics or eat too much junk food loaded with saturated fat (or both), cholesterol can clog our arteries, leaving us susceptible to a heart attack or stroke. Eating flaxseeds has been shown to help reverse high cholesterol. Why not sprinkle a few into every meal?

THE GRAPE FOUNDATION

MAKES 1 SERVING

Rich in vitamins A, B$_6$, and C, folate, iron, and selenium, grapes can tone and treat wrinkles and age spots. It's why adding grapes (and maybe a glass of wine or two) to your regular diet is great for your skin.

---

1 cup unsweetened
cashew milk

1 cup spinach

1 banana

½ cup frozen red
seedless grapes

2 tablespoons almond butter

1 tablespoon ground
flaxseeds*

In a blender, combine the cashew milk, spinach, banana, grapes, almond butter, and flaxseeds. Blend until the desired consistency is reached and enjoy!

Per serving: 426 calories, 24 g fat (2.5 g saturated fat), 50 g carbohydrates, 28 g sugar, 90 mg sodium, 9 g fiber, 10 g protein

✳ Flaxseeds are sold either whole or ground (also called flax meal). Although whole seeds have a longer shelf life, you will need to grind them yourself before adding them to a smoothie. Buy ground flax for quicker prep times.

COCOA GLOW SKIN SMOOTHIE

MAKES 1 SERVING

You won't necessarily taste the kale in this smoothie, but its high vitamin C content helps your body make the collagen required for skin strength and smoothness. Kale is also high in copper, a mineral that increases the production of melanin, a pigment that helps protect your skin from the sun. Combine that with the powerful antioxidants in the cacao and fruit, and you've got a deliciously healthy, skin-loving treat!

1 cup chopped kale

½ cup unsweetened almond milk or coconut water

½ cup blueberries

½ cup chopped pineapple

2 tablespoons unsweetened cacao powder or unsweetened cocoa powder

1 tablespoon natural nut butter

1 tablespoon ground flaxseeds (optional)

In a blender, combine the kale, almond milk or coconut water, blueberries, pineapple, cacao or cocoa powder, nut butter, and flaxseeds (if using). Blend until the desired consistency is reached. Serve over ice, if preferred.

Per serving: 362 calories, 17 g fat (5 g saturated fat), 44 g carbohydrates, 16 g sugar, 177 mg sodium, 14 g fiber, 15 g protein

WATER YOUR MELON SMOOTHIE

Like a face mask in a glass, this drink's loaded with the nutrients to hydrate and nourish your epidermis with healthy fats and B vitamins. At more than 80 percent water, this juicy melon flushes toxins to keep your complexion clear, while oranges supply a vitamin C payload to fuel collagen production.

1 cup chopped watermelon

1 banana

1 small avocado

1 orange, peeled and chopped

Handful of ice

In a blender, combine the watermelon, banana, avocado, orange, and ice. Blend until the desired consistency is reached and enjoy.

Per serving: 534 calories, 30 g fat (4.5 g saturated fat), 71 g carbohydrates, 37 g sugar, 19 mg sodium, 20 g fiber, 7 g protein

HONEYDEW COMPLEXION SMOOTHIE

MAKES 1 SERVING

This refreshing concoction is an aesthetician's dream: vitamin C, plumping potassium, skin cell–regenerating copper, and plenty of H_2O.

3 cups chopped honeydew melon

1 small green apple, peeled and sliced

1 cup spinach

1 fresh or frozen banana

2 kiwifruit

In a blender, combine the melon, apple, spinach, banana, and kiwifruit. Blend until smooth and serve.

Per serving: 454 calories, 2 g fat (0 g saturated fat), 115 g carbohydrates, 84 g sugar, 113 mg sodium, 15 g fiber, 7 g protein

Did you know?

One kiwifruit provides 100 percent of your daily vitamin C needs! This is critical for collagen synthesis and keeping the skin firm. Kiwis also have vitamin E, which helps reduce fine lines and wrinkles as well as the effects of ultraviolet radiation on the skin.

PACK YOUR (UNDER-EYE) BAGS SMOOTHIE

MAKES 1 SERVING

The secret ingredient in this smoothie is actually . . . parsley! Loaded with vitamins A, B, C, and K *and* the minerals iron and potassium, parsley helps reduce under-eye bags and darkness, and it speeds up the healing process of wounds and wrinkles. Romaine lettuce is also a sneaky way to get additional vitamins A and C, which build firm, healthy skin and prevent acne and inflammation.

1 cup coconut water

1 cup spinach or kale

3 leaves romaine lettuce

1 small lemon, peeled, seeded, and chopped

1 small pear, cut into pieces

½ cup frozen pineapple

4 sprigs parsley

2 tablespoons ground flaxseeds

In a blender, combine the coconut water, spinach or kale, lettuce, lemon, pear, pineapple, parsley, and flaxseeds. Blend until the desired consistency is reached and serve.

Per serving: 287 calories, 6 g fat (0.5 g saturated fat), 59 g carbohydrates, 37 g sugar, 68 mg sodium, 14 g fiber, 6 g protein

Parsley is a natural breath freshener. It reduces the odor of garlic breath when chewed fresh. This is due to parsley's high chlorophyll levels. The best way to keep fresh parsley sprigs is to wrap them in damp paper towels, place in a sealed zip-top bag, and refrigerate.

SO GOOD TO C YOU SMOOTHIE

MAKES 1 SERVING

Coconut water is not only totally delicious, it's an excellent source of magnesium and potassium, keeping you *and* your skin well hydrated. And since research shows that people who eat vitamin C–rich foods have fewer wrinkles and skin problems than those who don't, we've loaded this smoothie with free radical–fighting strawberries, mangoes, oranges, and nectarines.

1 cup coconut water

1 navel orange, peeled and chopped

1 cup fresh or frozen nectarine slices

1 cup chopped carrots

1 cup fresh or frozen mango chunks

1 cup fresh or frozen strawberries

In a blender, combine the coconut water, orange, nectarine, carrots, mango, and strawberries. Blend until the desired consistency is reached and enjoy!

Per serving: 373 calories, 2 g fat (0.5 g saturated fat), 92 g carbohydrates, 69 g sugar, 136 mg sodium, 15 g fiber, 7 g protein

Not only is frozen fruit cheaper, but according to the International Food Information Council, frozen fruit has just as much if not more nutritional value as fresh fruit. Fruits such as blueberries and strawberries are picked at their peak of freshness, then cleaned, packed, frozen, and sent right to the store. Fresh fruit often goes bad within days. Frozen fruit, however, lasts for months in the freezer. In addition, you don't have to wash and cut frozen fruit, which saves you time!

SAVING FACE SMOOTHIE BOWL

MAKES 2 SERVINGS

We love a good smoothie bowl! This one layers thick Greek yogurt with fruit, coconut, avocado, and spinach. Popeye knew what he was doing—the vitamin A in spinach helps retain moisture in the epidermis, combating psoriasis, keratinization, acne, and even wrinkles! It also helps skin repair itself and prevents dry, flaky skin.

1 cup spinach

1 small banana

½ avocado

½ cup sliced strawberries + additional for topping

½ cup blueberries + additional for topping

½ cup unsweetened almond milk (or more for a thinner consistency)

½ cup plain 2% Greek yogurt*

TOPPINGS

2 tablespoons slivered almonds

2 tablespoons shredded coconut

Small handful of berries

In a blender, combine the spinach, banana, avocado, ½ cup strawberries, ½ cup blueberries, almond milk, and yogurt. Blend until all ingredients are well incorporated, then pour into a bowl. Top with the almonds, coconut, and a few berries.

Per serving: 559 calories, 32 g fat (10 g saturated fat), 59 g carbohydrates, 30 g sugar, 155 mg sodium, 17 g fiber, 18 g protein

✳ Greek yogurt contains fewer carbohydrates, less sugar, and more protein than regular yogurt. Greek yogurt is also easier to digest than regular yogurt because the liquid whey (milk protein) has been separated out, giving it its thicker, creamier consistency.

Did you know?

If you're vegetarian, you may be deficient in vitamin B_{12}, which is mainly found in animal products. Greek yogurt is a healthy, easy way to get B_{12}.

TRADITIONAL TOMATO SOUP

Tomatoes contain a phytochemical called lycopene, which your body requires but does not produce—and it's an important carotenoid that fights free radicals and promotes skin firmness, elasticity, and smoothness. Cooking tomatoes actually concentrates the amount of lycopene, making it a more powerful antioxidant.

1 head garlic

14 Roma (plum) tomatoes, halved lengthwise

3 medium yellow onions, halved lengthwise

1½ tablespoons olive oil

Salt and ground black pepper

2½ cups water

1 cup unsweetened almond milk

1 tablespoon pure maple syrup

2 teaspoons paprika

2 teaspoons dried basil

1 teaspoon dried oregano

1. Preheat the oven to 400°F. Peel the outer skin from the entire garlic head. Cut the top of the garlic head off, exposing the tops of the cloves.

2. On a parchment-lined baking sheet, arrange the tomatoes, onions, and garlic, cut sides up. Drizzle with the oil and season to taste with salt and pepper.

3. Bake for 1 hour, checking to make sure that the garlic and onions do not burn. Remove the baking sheet from the oven and set it on a rack. When cooled, peel the garlic cloves.

4. In a large blender, combine the tomatoes and onions with their juices from the baking sheet, 7 of the peeled roasted garlic cloves, the water, almond milk, maple syrup, paprika, basil, and oregano. Puree until smooth.

5. Transfer the pureed soup to a large saucepan over medium heat and heat through before serving.

Per serving: 153 calories, 7 g fat (1 g saturated fat), 23 g carbohydrates, 13 g sugar, 139 mg sodium, 5 g fiber, 4 g protein

CLEAR COMPLEXION CARROT SOUP

MAKES 4 SERVINGS

Carrots give any dish a pop of color and satisfying crunch, but they're also great for keeping skin super vibrant. Our bodies convert the beta-carotene in carrots into vitamin A, which repairs skin damage and protects against harsh UV rays. Prevent premature aging with a diet full of bright orange skin savers.

3 tablespoons canola oil

2 teaspoons curry powder

8 large carrots, chopped

5 ribs celery, chopped

1 medium onion, chopped

5 cups low-sodium vegetable broth

Salt and ground black pepper

1. In a large saucepan over medium heat, warm the oil and curry powder. Stir for 2 minutes. Add the carrots, celery, and onion. Cook for about 10 minutes, stirring frequently.

2. Stir in the broth and bring to a boil. Reduce the heat and simmer for about 12 minutes, or until the vegetables are very tender. Remove from the heat and let stand for 15 minutes.

3. Working in batches, transfer the soup to a blender and puree until smooth.

4. Pour the pureed soup back into the saucepan, add salt and pepper to taste, and reheat the soup before serving.

Per serving: 203 calories, 11 g fat (1 g saturated fat), 23 g carbohydrates, 10 g sugar, 390 mg sodium, 6 g fiber, 2 g protein

CAULIFLOWER COLLAGEN-BOOSTING SOUP

This creamy, satisfying soup combines two veggies that are anything but boring! Cauliflower is chock-full of vitamin C, folate, fiber, and vitamin K, and broccoli boasts tons of vitamins C and E. Together they help boost collagen production, retain skin's moisture, and keep skin supple.

2 tablespoons olive oil

½ cup chopped onions

1 large clove garlic, minced

1 tablespoon chopped fresh cilantro stems

1 teaspoon curry powder

½ teaspoon ground turmeric

4 cups low-sodium vegetable or chicken broth

1 can (13–14 ounces) light coconut milk

2 cups broccoli florets

2 cups cauliflower florets

3 tablespoons whole grain mustard

1 tablespoon chopped fresh dill

Pinch of salt and ground black pepper

Juice of 1 lemon

1. In a large saucepan over medium heat, warm the oil. Cook the onions and garlic for 5 minutes, stirring frequently, or until softened. Stir in the cilantro, curry powder, and turmeric.

2. Add the broth, coconut milk, broccoli, and cauliflower. Increase the heat to high and bring to a boil, then reduce the heat to maintain a gentle simmer. Cover and simmer for 15 to 20 minutes, or until the vegetables are tender. Remove from the heat and cool slightly.

3. Working in batches, transfer the soup to a blender. Add the mustard, dill, salt, and pepper to one of the batches. Puree until smooth.

4. Return the soup to the pot, stir, and reheat. Add lemon juice to taste before serving.

Per serving: 188 calories, 12 g fat (5 g saturated fat), 17 g carbohydrates, 6 g sugar, 389 mg sodium, 4 g fiber, 3 g protein

GOTTA GLOW PUREE

MAKES 4 SERVINGS

This antioxidant-packed puree combines asparagus, fennel, kale, and spinach, which provide superhero levels of vitamins A, C, and E. And if you're a garlic lover, you're in luck: Garlic contains the antioxidant allicin, which fights wrinkles.

1 tablespoon canola oil

2 cups chopped asparagus

2 ribs celery, chopped

1 bulb fennel, chopped, fronds reserved for garnish

1 onion, finely chopped

2 cloves garlic, minced

1½ cups low-sodium vegetable broth

4–5 cups chopped kale

1 cup spinach

Juice of 1 lime

1. In a large saucepan over low heat, warm the oil. Add the asparagus, celery, fennel, onion, and garlic and cook, stirring, for about 5 minutes.

2. Add the broth, bring to a boil, then lower the heat and simmer for 10 minutes.

3. Add the kale and spinach. Remove the saucepan from the heat and let it cool slightly.

4. Working in batches, transfer the soup to a blender. Add the lime juice to one of the batches. Puree the soup until smooth.

5. Return the soup to the saucepan, reheat, garnish with a fennel frond, and serve warm.

Per serving: 123 calories, 4 g fat (0.5 g saturated fat), 19 g carbohydrates, 3 g sugar, 131 mg sodium, 6 g fiber, 6 g protein

Did you know?

Asparagus contains more folic acid than any other vegetable. It is also packed with fiber, potassium, and vitamins A, C, and E, all important for the skin. These antioxidants make asparagus one of the top fruits and vegetables to neutralize cell-damaging free radicals.

RADIANT RED PEPPER SOUP

MAKES 4 SERVINGS

Red bell peppers and tomatoes contain the antioxidant lycopene, which gives them their bright red pop of color. Lycopene is also a carotenoid that fights the free radicals your skin faces from exposure to damaging particles in the air.

1 red bell pepper, seeded and chopped

10 dry-packed sun-dried tomatoes, soaked in $\frac{1}{2}$ cup water (reserve the soaking water)

2 large carrots, chopped

$\frac{3}{4}$ cup water

$\frac{1}{4}$ cup raw cashews, soaked in water for 6 hours, then drained and rinsed

3 leaves fresh basil

In a blender, combine the bell pepper, tomatoes with their soaking water, carrots, water, cashews, and basil. Blend until the desired consistency is reached. Serve warm or chilled.

Per serving: 76 calories, 3 g fat (1 g saturated fat), 10 g carbohydrates, 5 g sugar, 41 mg sodium, 2 g fiber, 3 g protein

PLUMP-SKIN SOUP

MAKES 4 SERVINGS

It's time to switch up your Fall routine—pumpkin's not just for pies! In fact, a savory pumpkin dish like this fiber-rich soup will keep your skin soft and smooth. Pumpkin is packed with nutrients like vitamin C, beta-carotene, and carotenoids, which can help reverse UV damage and improve skin texture. Plus, the zinc in pumpkin helps maintain collagen. Buh-bye wrinkles!

2 tablespoons olive oil

1 cup chopped onion

3 cloves garlic, minced

3 cups canned pumpkin

2 cups low-sodium vegetable broth

1/2 teaspoon ground allspice

1 1/2 cups unsweetened coconut milk

Salt and ground black pepper

1. In a large saucepan over medium heat, warm the oil. Add the onion and garlic and cook, stirring frequently, for about 10 minutes.

2. Add the pumpkin, broth, and allspice. Bring to a boil, reduce the heat, then cover and simmer for about 30 minutes. Remove from the heat and set the soup aside to cool slightly.

3. Working in batches, transfer the soup to a blender and puree until smooth.

4. Return the soup to the saucepan. Bring the soup to a simmer and stir in the coconut milk. Season to taste with salt and pepper.

Per serving: 171 calories, 9 g fat (3 g saturated fat), 21 g carbohydrates, 8 g sugar, 160 mg sodium, 6 g fiber, 3 g protein

Chapter 3

All-Day Energy

Fuel Your Body Right

Some days you can wake up early, get a run in before work, pick up the dry cleaning, and eat a healthy, home-made dinner by 7:00 p.m. Other days, nothing gets done except binge-watching a few episodes (okay, a whole season) of *Game of Thrones*. That's life, right? The truth is, it's okay to give yourself a break, or even a whole day off. Sometimes the lack of energy you feel is your body telling you it needs rest or better nutrition. When we're too busy, we often forget about both. You wouldn't put cheap gas in a Lamborghini, right? Our bodies deserve the same care and respect. The cheaper or less healthy our food, the less fuel we have to keep moving, fight stress, and stay fit. Soups and smoothies with energy-boosting ingredients are like the high-octane gas of body fueling. Adding even just a few per week can keep your system humming smoothly.

YOU GOTTA EAT TO HAVE ENERGY

Every food and nutrient has a purpose, and it's our job to fuel our bodies with the right foods at the right times. Balancing the three main energy players—carbohydrates, protein, and fat—is key to maintaining your energy, mood, and overall health. A couple of major myths continue to persist despite the latest research: first, that carbs are the enemy. Not true! In fact, your brain runs on glucose. Healthy carbs like rice, fruit, starches, and oats are designed to feed your body the sugar it needs to function. Eliminating carbs from your diet is not a good idea. You'll end up eating more protein and fat than necessary, and protein is actually *not* intended to be used by your body for energy (myth #2). This will eventually lead to health problems. Proteins such as yogurt, nuts, chicken, cheese, and beans are designed to build muscle, repair tissues, and keep you fuller longer. Finally, fat doesn't make you fat! Let's put this myth to rest for good. Healthy fats such as avocados, olive oil, flaxseeds, and nuts are important to slow down digestion and give you a feeling of satiety.

KEY ENERGY PLAYERS

It's essential that we balance the quantity and timing of our intake of these nutrients so that we keep our blood sugar in check and promote steady energy, mood, and productivity levels. Eating more, but smaller, meals every 3 to 4 hours is recommended to prevent low blood sugar (read: *hanger*) and keep you going all day long. It also keeps you from eating huge portions at dinner or before bed.

Carbohydrates

Complex carbs are the supreme fuel for your body. They increase energy and elevate our mood by increasing serotonin, the "happy" neurotransmitter. You may feel better after downing a bag of potato chips, but it's a false high—your body will use up the simple carbs quickly and then crash again. But complex carbs like fruit, oats, and nuts provide hours of steady energy! The soup and smoothie recipes in this chapter combine delicious complex carbs with filling fat and protein to give your body the optimal fuel it craves.

Protein

Most energy comes from fast-burning carbohydrates, but you can't use that energy without adequate protein. Protein is the bedrock of a balanced diet. It helps maintain muscle and aids in the production of hormones and enzymes. It also helps keep blood sugar even so it doesn't spike erratically. Keeping a container of almonds or walnuts around is a great idea: Nuts are one of the best energy boosters since they contain healthy fats, protein, vitamin E, and magnesium, a mineral that plays a significant role in transforming sugar into energy. The key is keeping your intake to a handful or so.

Hungry before bed? Grab a snack high in protein and low in carbs; this keeps blood glucose levels stable so you don't get an unexpected kick of energy. Great go-to's are a piece of hard cheese (or string cheese) and a handful of crackers, an apple with 1 tablespoon of almond butter, a slice of whole grain toast with 1 tablespoon almond butter, or Greek yogurt topped with $\frac{1}{4}$ cup granola. Don't opt for snacks high in sugar either, or you'll be in for an unwanted jolt of energy.

Fat

For years we've been told that the key to being healthy is eating a low-fat diet. But not all fat is created equal. In reality, it's more about the *kind* of fat you're eating. Experts now recommend diets high in *healthy* fats, which are found in foods such as avocado, olive oil, eggs, and nuts. These good fats help maintain steady blood sugar levels, keep you full, and are packed with nutrients that also give you healthy skin and nails.

Fiber

Another component critical to sustaining energy and steady blood sugar is fiber. Fiber slows digestion, which keeps you fuller longer and energizes you throughout the day. That's why most processed foods and snacks like chips and candy keep you satiated for only a short time—they lack the all-important fiber found in better options like fruits, veggies, whole grains, and beans. Check out Busy "B" Soup on page 77 for a fiber-rich energy boost.

Caffeine

It may not be news that dark chocolate is good for you, but do you know why?

It's packed with antioxidants and contains caffeine, which elevates our energy and mood. It also contains theobromine, a natural stimulant similar to caffeine, which also keeps you more alert and awake. Not to mention that eating small amounts of dark chocolate is a healthy way to satisfy sweet cravings! Another great source of caffeine is green tea, which is also loaded with disease-fighting antioxidants and catechin. It boosts metabolism, promotes healthy weight, improves brain function, and lowers the risk of cancer. What's not to love? Brew up a pot, let it cool, and serve the tea over ice with a bit of honey or agave for a refreshingly healthy summer drink.

Now, most of us depend on a morning cup of coffee—sometimes two. Coffee is a caffeine superstar. It increases energy and improves mood, memory, and cognitive function. It's sometimes the only reason we can get out of bed in the morning! Just remember: Don't rely on caffeine too much. Yes, it's great for a quick boost, but it can leave you crashing. For a nice morning fix, check out the incredibly delicious, energy-boosting Wake Up and Go Smoothie on page 68.

TRUE OR FALSE: SUGAR FUELS YOUR BODY

True, but we don't mean cake and ice cream! Our bodies run on glucose, or the concentration of sugar in our blood. Glucose is made by the breakdown of all food, which travels throughout the body via our bloodstream and enters into cells with the help of insulin. Without insulin, the cells cannot use glucose, so it hangs out in our bloodstream, causing high blood sugar and diabetes. Some foods are great at maintaining steady blood sugar; others, not so much. The recipes in this chapter focus on the best foods to keep your glucose level balanced and keep you feeling energized and happy.

We know that too much sugar in our blood is bad for us, but too little can also be dangerous. When your blood sugar levels fall too low—you skip a meal, exercise without enough fuel, or wait too long to eat—you may experience hypoglycemia, which can become a medical emergency. Hypoglycemia can be mistaken for many other common ailments, so it's good to know the symptoms. Fortunately, the soups and smoothies in this book are full of all the right nutrients to make sure you're keeping balanced blood sugar levels. It's our foolproof, no-crash guarantee.

HACK YOUR HYPOGLYCEMIA
Symptoms

- Headache
- Shakiness, anxiety, nervousness
- Palpitations, tachycardia
- Sweating, feeling of warmth
- Hunger, stomachache
- Nausea, vomiting, abdominal discomfort

- Abnormal thinking, impaired judgment
- Irritability
- Fatigue, weakness, lethargy
- Confusion, memory loss, lightheadedness or dizziness, delirium

Quick Treatments

If you find yourself experiencing any hypoglycemic symptoms and it's been a while since you ate, or you just finished an intense workout, here are some easy ways to quickly bring your glucose levels back to normal.

If you are experiencing hypoglycemia, eat or drink 15 grams of rapidly digesting carbohydrates, such as:

- ½ cup of fruit juice
- 1 cup of nonfat milk
- 5 saltine crackers

- 1 tablespooon of honey
- 1 cup of Gatorade or another sports drink

Fun facts about …
CACAO

What Makes Cacao So Cool?

Cacao is so trendy these days—it even had its own cameo on *Portlandia*. That's probably because as the world grows ever more health conscious, superfoods become more popular. It's also a good source of caffeine—not as strong as coffee, but good for a slight bump in energy.

Cacao can be added to almost any of our smoothies for a rich, chocolaty flavor boost and pick-me-up.

HEALTH PERK

Cacao nibs are essentially the purest form of chocolate. They're made by roasting the seeds of the cacao tree and have a bitter, nutty flavor, like a cross between chocolate and coffee.

Nourishing Cacao Yogurt Facial Mask

For a twist on your next Friday night in, why not try a cacao facial? The natural antioxidants found in cacao can be consumed or applied topically to banish free radicals and repair skin cells. This cleansing facial mask combines antioxidant-rich cacao powder and antimicrobial manuka honey (if you can't find this New Zealand variety, regular honey offers similar benefits). Yogurt provides a creamy texture and probiotics, which soothe skin irritation when applied topically.

> ⅓ cup organic cacao powder
>
> 3 tablespoons plain yogurt
>
> 1 tablespoon manuka or regular honey
>
> ½–2 teaspoons water (optional)
>
> Squeeze of lemon juice

In a bowl, combine the cacao powder and yogurt, stirring until a paste forms. Add the honey and continue to mix until blended thoroughly. Make a thinner mask by mixing in the water, a bit at a time, if desired. Squeeze some lemon juice into the mixture for added antibacterial power and for a natural preservative. The added lemon juice allows you to store the mask in the refrigerator for a few days. Apply a thin layer of the mask to your face and leave it on for 5 to 10 minutes. Wash thoroughly with warm water, and enjoy your soft, glowing skin!

Boost Your Mood

Cacao is delicious and it promotes cardiovascular health, skin health, and blood pressure stability. Studies have shown that cacao can also help boost your endorphin and serotonin levels, while boosting energy. Who can say no to that?

CURBS CRAVINGS

Did you know that even just the *smell* of cacao can activate the same neurotransmitters that are stimulated when you eat chocolate? That means you can use the scent to curb cravings! But cacao has such great health benefits, you can smell your cake and eat it too. The small amount of caffeine can also help with pesky cravings while giving you extra pep on a sleepy day.

POWER NUT BUTTER BOWL

This ultra-satisfying smoothie bowl combines healthy carbs, protein, fat, and a little caffeine to rev your engine in the morning and keep you going all day long. The nut butter and nuts provide protein and healthy fats to slow digestion of the carbs and stabilize your blood sugar for hours after you've skipped out the front door.

1 cup unsweetened coconut milk, cashew milk, or almond milk

1 large fresh or frozen banana

2 tablespoons natural nut butter

1 tablespoon unsweetened cocoa powder

¼ teaspoon vanilla extract

Handful of ice

TOPPINGS

2 tablespoons granola

2 tablespoons chopped walnuts or almonds

2 tablespoons cacao nibs

1 tablespoon chia seeds or flaxseeds (optional)

Shredded coconut (optional)

In a blender, combine the milk, banana, nut butter, cocoa powder, vanilla, and ice. Blend until the desired consistency is reached. Pour the smoothie into a bowl and sprinkle it with the granola, chopped nuts, cacao nibs, and chia seeds or flaxseeds, if using.

Per serving: 690 calories, 46 g fat (12 g saturated fat), 63 g carbohydrates, 24 g sugar, 112 mg sodium, 19 g fiber, 18 g protein

WAKE UP AND GO SMOOTHIE

MAKES 1 SERVING

This is the ultimate chocolatey-coffee morning treat! The coffee and cacao provide energizing caffeine, the banana and fiber-rich oats fuel your body, and the nut butter slows digestion, sending you out the door ready to take on the world (or, at least, your morning commute).

1 fresh or frozen banana

½ cup cold coffee

½ cup unsweetened almond milk or coconut milk

¼ cup rolled (old-fashioned) oats

1 tablespoon natural nut butter

1 teaspoon cacao nibs, for garnish

In a blender, combine the banana, coffee, milk, oats, and nut butter. (If the banana is not frozen, you may want to add a handful of ice for a thicker consistency.) Blend until the desired consistency is reached. Serve sprinkled with the cacao nibs on top.

Per serving: 489 calories, 29 g fat (3 g saturated fat), 50 g carbohydrates, 18 g sugar, 200 mg sodium, 10 g fiber, 14 g protein

✳ If you're not a big breakfast eater or all that hungry first thing in the morning, smoothies are a great way to fuel up without feeling weighed down.

GREEN ENERGY SMOOTHIE

MAKES 1 SERVING

This supergreen combo mixes energizing carbs, protein, and fiber to propel you forward without crashes or cravings. Flaxseeds add additional fiber to help slow digestion and keep you fuller longer.

1 cup unsweetened almond milk, coconut milk, or cashew milk

1 cup chopped kale

1 pear, cored and chopped

1 fresh or frozen banana

1 tablespoon almond butter or peanut butter

1 tablespoon flaxseeds

Ice as needed (omit if the banana is frozen)

In a blender, combine the milk, kale, pear, banana, nut butter, flaxseeds, and ice (if using). Blend until the desired consistency is reached and enjoy.

Per serving: 431 calories, 17 g fat (2 g saturated fat), 68 g carbohydrates, 33 g sugar, 247 mg sodium, 15 g fiber, 11 g protein

Pears ripen at room temperature, so place them on the kitchen counter or on the dining room table in a pretty bowl to double as room décor as they ripen. Placing them in a paper bag will speed up the ripening process. Ripening fruit gives off ethylene, and more ethylene in the air around the pears will make them ripen faster; therefore, you can add apples or bananas to the bowl or bag to further speed up the process. When the pears are ripe, store them in the refrigerator to keep them just at the right ripeness for blending!

GREEN TEA SMOOTHIE

MAKES 1 SERVING

A perfect alternative to your morning joe, green tea has enough caffeine to keep you energized and alert for whatever the day brings. Combined with honeydew and avocado, it makes a refreshingly delicious smoothie that just could become addictive!

2 cups chopped honeydew melon

¾ cup brewed green tea (use 2 tea bags and steep for about 10 minutes to make it strong)

1 small avocado

¼ cup unsweetened almond milk or cashew milk

1 teaspoon honey

In a blender, combine the melon, tea, avocado, milk, and honey. Blend until the desired consistency is reached and sip away!

Per serving: 259 calories, 2 g fat (0.5 g saturated fat), 64 g carbohydrates, 48 g sugar, 108 mg sodium, 6 g fiber, 3 g protein

OAT-NUT SMOOTHIE

MAKES 2 SERVINGS

Like a parfait in a glass, this smoothie blends thick, creamy Greek yogurt and almond butter, a filling combo of protein, carbs, fat, and fiber.

---

1 cup plain or vanilla 2% Greek yogurt

1 fresh or frozen banana

½ cup unsweetened coconut milk or almond milk

¼ cup rolled (old-fashioned) oats

2 tablespoons almond butter

Honey, to taste

Ice as needed

In a blender, combine the yogurt, banana, coconut or almond milk, oats, almond butter, honey to taste, and ice. Blend until fully mixed, and serve.

Per serving: 543 calories, 24 g fat (5 g saturated fat), 61 g carbohydrates, 32 g sugar, 147 mg sodium, 8 g fiber, 29 g protein

Did you know?

There are about 60,000 bees in a beehive that collectively travel up to 55,000 miles and visit more than 2 million flowers to accumulate enough nectar to make just 1 pound of honey! The color and flavor of honey depend on the bees' nectar source (the blossoms). There are more than 300 unique types of honey in the United States, originating from floral sources such as clover, eucalyptus, and orange blossoms. Lighter-colored honeys have a mild flavor, whereas darker honeys are more robust in flavor.

CRANBERRY ALMOND PROTEIN SMOOTHIE

MAKES 1 SERVING

Almond butter and Greek yogurt are high in protein to help stabilize blood sugars and prevent the dreaded late-afternoon "crash." The berries and juice offer up healthy carbs to boost energy levels and fuel your body all day long.

$\frac{1}{2}$ **cup frozen cranberries**

2 tablespoons almond butter

$\frac{1}{2}$ **cup unsweetened cranberry juice**

$\frac{1}{2}$ **cup plain 2% Greek yogurt**

$\frac{1}{2}$ **cup blackberries**

In a blender, combine the cranberries, almond butter, cranberry juice, yogurt, and blackberries. Blend until slightly chunky. If you prefer a thinner smoothie, add more cranberry juice.

Per serving: 381 calories, 20 g fat (4 g saturated fat), 39 g carbohydrates, 27 g sugar, 112 mg sodium, 9 g fiber, 18 g protein

CHICKPEA ENERGY SOUP

MAKES 4 SERVINGS

The simple chickpea shines here as a terrific source of both protein and fiber, keeping you energized and satisfied. Its costar is the equally humble potato, which is an excellent source of complex carbs.

2 tablespoons olive oil

1 small onion, chopped

1 clove garlic, minced

1 rib celery, chopped

1 carrot, chopped

3 cups low-sodium vegetable broth

2 russet potatoes, peeled and cubed

2 cans (14.5 ounces each) diced tomatoes, undrained

2 cans (15 ounces each) chickpeas, drained and rinsed

2 tablespoons garam masala

½ teaspoon ground turmeric

Salt and ground black pepper

1. In a large stockpot over medium-high heat, warm the oil. Add the onion, garlic, celery, and carrot and cook, stirring frequently, for 5 minutes, or until soft.

2. Add the vegetable broth, potatoes, tomatoes and their juices, chickpeas, garam masala, and turmeric and simmer for 30 minutes, stirring occasionally.

3. Remove from the heat and add salt and pepper to taste.

4. Puree half of the soup in a blender and return it to the pot. Heat the soup through and serve warm.

Per serving: 402 calories, 9 g fat (1 g saturated fat), 71 g carbohydrates, 4 g sugar, 10 mg sodium, 9 g fiber, 10 g protein

Did you know?

The spices typically used to make garam masala include coriander, cumin, cardamom, mustard seeds, bay leaves, fennel, fenugreek, caraway, black and white peppercorns, cloves, mace, nutmeg, and cinnamon. Garam masala's health benefits include boosting immunity, improving digestion, supporting weight loss, relieving pain, and decreasing blood sugar levels.

MOTIVATING (MEATLESS) BEAN SOUP

MAKES 4 SERVINGS

Beans may sound boring, but they provide carbohydrates, protein, *and* fiber for lasting energy throughout the day (and they're cholesterol free)! Beans are also a great way to give your body a rest from animal proteins, which are harder to digest than vegetable proteins. Whip up this easy, savory soup on Meatless Mondays and your body will thank you (possibly out loud).

¼ cup olive oil

4 cups chopped yellow onions (about 2 large)

2 cloves garlic, minced

3 cans (15 ounces each) cannellini or great northern beans, rinsed and drained

6 cups low-sodium vegetable broth

2 bay leaves

½ teaspoon dried thyme

1. In a large stockpot over medium-high heat, warm the oil. Add the onions and cook, stirring frequently, for 5 minutes, or until soft. Add the garlic and cook, stirring, for 5 minutes.

2. Add the beans, broth, bay leaves, and thyme and bring to a boil. Then turn down the heat and simmer for about 20 minutes.

3. Remove the soup from the heat, and remove the bay leaves.

4. Using an immersion blender, carefully purée the soup until smooth. Or puree in batches in a regular blender.

Per serving: 315 calories, 14 g fat (2 g saturated fat), 45 g carbohydrates, 2 g sugar, 383 mg sodium, 9 g fiber, 8 g protein

❋ For extra flavor, top with crumbled veggie bacon.

BUSY "B" SOUP

MAKES 4 SERVINGS

It may not look that exciting, but cauliflower contains many B-complex vitamins such as folate, pantothenic acid (vitamin B_5), pyridoxine (vitamin B_6), thiamin (vitamin B_1), and niacin (B_3), as well as vitamin K. These vitamins all help boost metabolism, making this creamy, comforting soup a go-to during those extra-busy weeks.

2 tablespoons olive oil

1 onion, chopped

2 carrots, chopped

2 ribs celery, chopped

3 cloves garlic, minced

1 teaspoon curry powder

$\frac{1}{2}$ teaspoon ground turmeric

6 cups low-sodium vegetable broth

1 head cauliflower, chopped

1 russet potato, peeled and chopped

1. In a large stockpot over medium-high heat, warm the oil. Add the onion, carrots, celery, garlic, curry powder, and turmeric. Cook, stirring frequently, for 5 minutes, or until the onion is translucent.

2. Add the broth, cauliflower, and potato. Bring to a boil, then reduce the heat and simmer, covered, on low heat for 30 minutes, or until the vegetables are soft. Remove from the heat and let the soup cool slightly.

3. Working in batches, add the soup to a blender and puree it until smooth, or puree all of it at once using an immersion blender.

Per serving: 234 calories, 8 g fat (1 g saturated fat), 36 g carbohydrates, 8 g sugar, 298 mg sodium, 7 g fiber, 6 g protein

GLOWING VITALITY GAZPACHO

MAKES 4 SERVINGS

This funky, delicious twist on a chilled veggie soup combines superstar ingredients that fill you up without slowing you down. You can make a batch and keep it in the fridge for up to 3 days, or freeze it and thaw in the fridge overnight before serving, making this a perfectly cool summertime meal.

1 head romaine lettuce, coarsely chopped

1½ cups water

1 cup baby spinach

1 cucumber, peeled and chopped

1 green apple, seeded and chopped

1 avocado

¾ cup cherry tomatoes

½ cup fresh cilantro

1 lemon, peeled and quartered

1 clove garlic

In a blender, combine the lettuce, water, spinach, cucumber, apple, avocado, tomatoes, cilantro, lemon, and garlic. Pulse several times, then blend until smooth and creamy.

Per serving: 150 calories, 8 g fat (1 g saturated fat), 20 g carbohydrates, 9 g sugar, 33 mg sodium, 8 g fiber, 4 g protein

Did you know?

An overly acidic diet can sap your energy, increase the chance of obesity, and contribute to other health problems. Among its other awesome benefits, spinach contains minerals that balance the acid in our bodies.

SWEETS & BEETS SOUP

MAKES 4 SERVINGS

Sweet potatoes not only add flavor to a soup, they provide carbohydrates *and* fiber, which means they have a low glycemic index and release sugar slowly into the bloodstream. They're also an excellent source of manganese, which helps the body metabolize carbohydrates.

1 tablespoon olive oil

1 cup chopped onions

4 cups low-sodium vegetable broth

3 cups peeled, chopped sweet potatoes

2 cups peeled, chopped beets*

2 cups chopped carrots

½ cup chopped fresh parsley

2 teaspoons paprika

1 teaspoon garlic powder

Salt and ground black pepper

1. In a large stockpot over medium heat, warm the oil. Cook the onions, stirring frequently, for 5 to 7 minutes, or until golden brown.

2. Add the broth, sweet potatoes, beets, and carrots. Bring to a boil, cover, and simmer for 30 minutes, or until the vegetables are soft.

3. Add the parsley, paprika, and garlic powder. Puree the soup in the pot using an immersion blender, or puree it in batches using a standard blender. Season to taste with salt and pepper.

Per serving: 209 calories, 4 g fat (1 g saturated fat), 40 g carbohydrates, 14 g sugar, 368 mg sodium, 8 g fiber, 4 g protein

✳ Beets are beautiful—but they can also stain clothes and tablecloths! It's not a bad idea to don an apron while cooking this soup (or, at least, to stir *very* carefully).

Did you know?

Beets boost energy levels because they contain nitrates, which dilate blood vessels, leading to increased bloodflow—which makes your muscles work harder and boosts energy levels.

Brain Power

Feed Your Mind

When we think about nutrition, we usually think of the *body*. We might clean up our fridge and stock up on healthy foods to get our bods in shape for summer, to cure a cold, or to be more productive. But what about our *brains*? Your brain is the command center for your body and has its own specific nutritional needs. What you eat—and what you *don't* eat—affects your focus, mood, productivity, and overall quality of life. For example, getting the right vitamins can fight brain fog, memory loss, and even depression. In this chapter, you'll get a handle on what foods your brain needs to function at its best and keep you feeling super sharp.

COGNITIVE CURES

Peak mental health is crucial to living your happiest, healthiest, fullest life. We've all had days when we just felt tired, cranky, or in a funk—but a prolonged state of moodiness or forgetfulness is *no bueno*. You can stave off the blahs by taking care of your brain just as you take care of the rest of your body. Start to pay attention to how you feel when you eat certain foods (and we don't mean the obvious burrito bloat). Keep a food diary over a couple of days, and track your overall mood and productivity along with your meals. Are you energized, focused, and productive or tired, irritable, and headachy?

Chances are, you'll notice that there's a relationship between certain foods and certain moods. Your brain needs glucose in the form of carbohydrates—we'll show you which ones are healthiest—and it also needs proper rest and relaxation (hint: step away from the screen). Blend up a few of these recipes and you'll soon start to feel as focused as a laser.

Get Focused

Ever find yourself staring off into space on a busy afternoon? One of the ultimate powers of the human mind is its ability to focus for a prolonged period of time. But many of us struggle to concentrate, and pretty soon *everything* seems to take forever. An inability to concentrate can be a sign that your brain isn't getting the nutrients it needs. Part of the problem is that we tend to eat too many processed foods, which can be full of chemicals that inhibit brain function. The key is to replace all the packaged stuff with real, fresh (and really delicious) foods. Your brain craves vitamins, antioxidants, and phytonutrients, and fruits and vegetables are loaded with them. Adding a few soups and smoothies to your weekly meal plan can make all the difference in boosting your brain's abilities. Start loading up on the brain-boosting recipes in this chapter to make sure you're checking off all your to-do's with ease.

Eat Happy

A mood is simply your emotional state, and it can range from positively overjoyed (promotion! vacation!) to absolutely miserable (PMS, utter heartbreak). Our moods are easily

SIGNS AND SYMPTOMS OF DEPRESSION

If you have been experiencing some of the following signs and symptoms most of the day, every day, for at least 2 weeks, you may be suffering from depression and should seek out a mental health professional.

- Persistent sad, anxious, or "empty" mood

- Feelings of hopelessness

- Irritability

- Feelings of guilt, worthlessness, or helplessness

- Loss of interest or pleasure in hobbies and activities

- Decreased energy or feelings of fatigue

- Slower than normal movements or speech

- Difficulty concentrating, remembering, or making decisions

- Difficulty sleeping, early-morning awakening, or oversleeping

- Appetite and/or weight changes

- Aches or pains, headaches, cramps, or digestive problems without a clear cause or that do not ease with treatment

affected by what we put into our bodies, and we often use unhealthy food as emotional comfort. As clichéd as it sounds, we've all stared down that pint of ice cream or fast-food drive-thru after a particularly tough day. But the opposite is also true: After eating fresh food or exercising, the world sparkles in front of us! That's because certain foods (and workouts) increase levels of dopamine—the neurotransmitter that stokes our pleasure centers and makes us happier.

Fight Depression

More serious than mood swings, depression is one of the most common mental disorders, with more than 40 million sufferers in the United States, according to the National Institute of Mental Health. Depression is caused by a combination of genetic, biological, environmental, and psychological factors, and its symptoms can manifest in the way you feel, think, and handle daily activities, such as sleeping, eating, or working.

While prescription drugs can be effective, they are often costly, with many potentially dangerous side effects. Along with treatment, proper nutrition can be a powerful tool in the fight against depression. For example, low levels of folate can result in depressive symptoms, but folate-rich foods like dark leafy greens, asparagus, Brussels sprouts, nuts, beans, peas, and oranges can help keep your energy levels up and promote a positive sense of well-being.

Ease Headaches

A pounding noggin is never fun, but the intensity and cause of the problem can range from a tension headache (a dull, constant pressure, especially at the temples or back of your neck) to the all-consuming tsunami of pain that is a migraine (see "How Do You Know You Have a Migraine?" for more symptoms). Headaches can often be a sign of dehydration, but they can also be an indicator of poor nutrition—for example, if you're filling up on too many sweets or processed foods. Try the Take Two and Call Me in the Morning Smoothie on page 92. Cherries are high in anthocyanins, which reduce inflammation and can help keep your head pain-free.

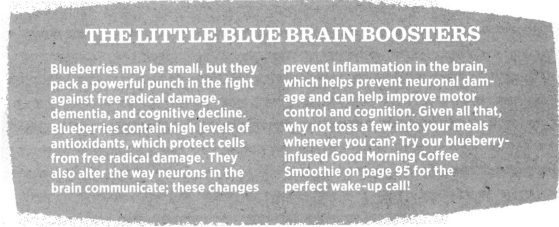

THE LITTLE BLUE BRAIN BOOSTERS

Blueberries may be small, but they pack a powerful punch in the fight against free radical damage, dementia, and cognitive decline. Blueberries contain high levels of antioxidants, which protect cells from free radical damage. They also alter the way neurons in the brain communicate; these changes prevent inflammation in the brain, which helps prevent neuronal damage and can help improve motor control and cognition. Given all that, why not toss a few into your meals whenever you can? Try our blueberry-infused Good Morning Coffee Smoothie on page 95 for the perfect wake-up call!

MIGRAINE SOLUTIONS

If you suffer from migraines you know you'd do anything to avoid one. The good news is there are some easy steps you can take to prevent a migraine. For starters, avoid drinking too much alcohol or caffeine, both of which set us up for painful crashes. Limit caffeine intake to 200 mg a day—that's about one 8-ounce cup of coffee. When it comes to alcohol, some people do fine with vodka instead of beer, according to Michael Blumenfeld, MD, director of the Headache Center of Southern California.

Another cause of migraines is a fluctuation in blood sugar. To avoid a blood sugar drop, don't go longer than 3 hours without food. Our smoothies and soups are a quick and easy way to ensure getting enough nutrients to avoid this type of crash.

Finally, don't skip out on sleep. A 2010 study found that sleep-deprived rats experienced changes to their migraine-related proteins. That means it's essential to be consistent about when you go to bed and when you get up. Treating your body with the utmost care is the best way to treat and prevent painful migraines.

Fun facts about ...
POMEGRANATES

Jewel of the Grocery Aisle

Next time you're in the produce section of the supermarket, you might consider buying a pomegranate, the vibrant red fruit with the juicy seeds inside. Pomegranate seeds, or arils, are chock-full of antioxidants such as polyphenol and tannins, which protect cells from free radical damage and can help improve cognitive skills and slow brain aging. Each small seed is packed with big, juicy flavor! We recommend putting them in any smoothie (or sprinkling them on top of smoothie bowls or salads) for a touch of sweetness, eye-catching color, and brain-boosting benefits.

Pomegranates were cool way before they started popping up at your local market. In fact, according to National Public Radio, they were used all the way back in 3000 BC. King Tut and other Egyptians were buried with pomegranates, to aid in their passage to the afterlife!

How to Open a Pomegranate

1.
Slice off the top and remove the flower.

2.
Use a knife to score the sides.

3.
Break open the pomegranate over a bowl.

4.
Free the seeds and discard the membrane.

BEYOND BRAIN HEALTH

They're called a superfood for a reason: Not only do pomegranates do wonders for your gray matter, they also boost your overall well-being. Here are just a few of their perks:

A NATURAL CHOLESTEROL BLOCKER

According to scientists at the Technion-Israel Institute of Technology, pomegranate is believed to have anti-atherogenic qualities. That means it can stop harmful plaque buildup in our blood vessels, caused by anything from smoking to eating too many saturated fats. By eating pomegranate seeds or drinking pomegranate juice, you can decrease your LDL or "bad" cholesterol buildup. This little shift in your diet could prevent a heart attack or stroke—so you can live smarter, better, and longer. That's one powerful little seed!

A BRIGHTER SNACK

Pomegranate seeds are loaded with fiber, which helps keep you satisfied—keep a bowl of them handy on your desk as an office treat (and a pretty pop of color). If the seeds alone aren't your thing, you can add a splash of concentrated pomegranate juice to your water or seltzer to score a hit of flavor and anti-inflammatory properties as you're hydrating.

TAKE TWO AND CALL ME IN THE MORNING SMOOTHIE

MAKES 1 SERVING

Cherries are high in anthocyanins, the bioflavonoids that give cherries their red, purple, and blue pigments. Their antioxidant and anti-inflammatory properties can help ease headache pain. Ginger also helps reduce inflammation, and chia seeds are high in omega-3 fatty acids, which keep the brain's arteries clear of plaque and support communication between brain cells.

1 cup frozen cherries, pitted

2 kiwifruits, chopped

¾ cup unsweetened almond milk or coconut milk

1 tablespoon chia seeds

1 teaspoon ground ginger

In a blender, combine the cherries, kiwis, milk, chia seeds, and ginger. Blend until the desired consistency is reached and enjoy!

Per serving: 261 calories, 6 g fat (0 g saturated fat), 49 g carbohydrates, 31 g sugar, 141 mg sodium, 12 g fiber, 5 g protein

GOOD MORNING COFFEE SMOOTHIE

MAKES 1 SERVING

The brain requires large amounts of oxygen and glucose to function properly, and bananas are high in glucose and other natural sugars that feed it quick energy. Bananas are also an excellent source of vitamin B_6, which the brain requires for energy metabolism and for making chemicals called neurotransmitters. Vitamin B_6 deficiency can cause problems including chronic pain, headache, and seizures—so this vitamin-packed smoothie is the perfect way to start your day out right.

---

1 cup unsweetened almond milk, coconut milk, or cashew milk

1 frozen banana

$\frac{1}{2}$ cup coffee, chilled

$\frac{1}{2}$ cup blueberries

2 tablespoons unsweetened cacao powder

$\frac{1}{4}$ teaspoon ground cinnamon

In a blender, combine the milk, banana, coffee, blueberries, cacao powder, and cinnamon. Blend until the desired consistency is reached and enjoy!

Per serving: 217 calories, 6 g fat (1.5 g saturated fat), 45 g carbohydrates, 22 g sugar, 184 mg sodium, 10 g fiber, 5 g protein

Did you know?

Bananas contain the amino acid tryptophan, a brain chemical that regulates mood—the same one that can make you sleepy after a Thanksgiving turkey dinner!

EINSTEIN SMOOTHIE

MAKES 1 SERVING

Sixty percent of the brain is made up of fat—and the healthy fats found in nut butters like peanut, almond, and cashew butter are critical for optimal brain health. Want to boost your brain power? Blend up this sweet and creamy treat.

1 cup unsweetened
almond milk

1 cup chopped kale or spinach

1 frozen banana

2 tablespoons natural
nut butter

2 tablespoons unsweetened
cacao powder

1 tablespoon ground
flaxseeds

In a blender, combine the almond milk, kale or spinach, banana, nut butter, cacao powder, and flaxseeds. Blend until the desired consistency is reached and enjoy!

Per serving: 445 calories, 25 g fat (4 g saturated fat), 49 g carbohydrates, 16 g sugar, 207 mg sodium, 12 g fiber, 16 g protein

Did you know?

Not only is dark chocolate (or cacao) a delicious way to satisfy your sweet tooth, it's also high in antioxidants and reduces levels of the stress hormone cortisol, making it a natural antidepressant.

DE-STRESSING DATE SMOOTHIE

MAKES 2 SERVINGS

Potassium is a critical mineral that normalizes the heartbeat, sends oxygen to the brain, and regulates the body's water balance. The high potassium levels in bananas and dates help decrease stress. Coconut water is a tasty way to replenish electrolyte levels and keep you calm and focused.

2 frozen bananas

1 cup chopped fresh or frozen mango

1 cup seeded, chopped cucumber

1 cup coconut water

3 ribs celery

3 Medjool dates, pitted

1 tablespoon ground flaxseeds

In a blender, combine the bananas, mango, cucumber, coconut water, celery, dates, and flaxseeds. Blend until the desired consistency is reached and enjoy!

Per serving: 650 calories, 5 g fat (1 g saturated fat), 157 g carbohydrates, 115 g sugar, 354 mg sodium, 27 g fiber, 10 g protein

Mango is high in B vitamins, which alleviate stress, tension, and depression. It is also loaded with magnesium, which feeds the nerve cells, inhibits depression, reduces the effects of stress, and regulates sleep. Eat more and you may feel like you've come back well rested from a tropical vacation!

CINNAMON SPICE BRAIN BOOSTER

A little sprinkling of cinnamon can go a long way when it comes to brain power. Researchers at Rush University found that this simple spice is converted into sodium benzoate, which promotes the neurons essential to learning and memory. Time to drink up and get sharp!

¼ cup raw cashews, soaked in water overnight*

1½ cups unsweetened almond milk or coconut milk

⅓ cup rolled (old-fashioned) oats

Handful of ice

1 tablespoon honey or agave nectar

1½ teaspoons ground cinnamon

1 teaspoon ground turmeric

Drain the cashews and transfer to a blender. Add the almond or coconut milk, oats, ice, honey or agave nectar, cinnamon, and turmeric. Blend until the desired consistency is reached and serve.

Per serving: 405 calories, 19 g fat (2 g saturated fat), 51 g carbohydrates, 20 g sugar, 277 mg sodium, 8 g fiber, 12 g protein

✳ A strong blender should be able to blend the cashews, but soaking them overnight softens them to ensure creaminess when blended. If you don't have cashews, you can substitute a frozen banana or 2 tablespoons cashew butter.

TAKE IT E-Z SMOOTHIE

MAKES 2 SERVINGS

This sweet little smoothie does double duty: It helps lift your mood and keeps you satisfied. Plus, the nuts and cacao contain vitamin E, an antioxidant that can help to stop cognitive decline as you age.

2 tablespoons cashew butter

2 tablespoons unsweetened natural cacao powder

1 frozen banana

2 Medjool dates, pitted

1 cup unsweetened cashew milk

1 teaspoon vanilla extract

In a blender, combine the cashew butter, cacao or cocoa powder, banana, dates, cashew milk, and vanilla. Blend until completely smooth.

Per serving: 603 calories, 48 g fat (7 g saturated fat), 86 g carbohydrates, 48 g sugar, 157 mg sodium, 15 g fiber, 15 g protein

Did you know?

Studies have shown that chocolate (cacao) affects your mood by raising the level of serotonin, a feel-good brain chemical. Cacao also contains a neurotransmitter called theobromine that releases the compound anandamide, which produces feelings of relaxation and contentment.

STAY SHARP SPINACH SOUP

MAKES 4 SERVINGS

A group of researchers at Rush University in Chicago who analyzed the diets and mental functions of 954 elderly people over a 5-year period found that those who incorporated more greens into their diets were more likely to be mentally sharp. Spinach contains vitamin K, which slows the process of age-related cognitive decline, and it's also high in nutrients that prevent dementia, like folate and vitamin E.

2 tablespoons olive oil

2 cups spinach

1½ cups low-sodium vegetable broth

1 avocado

2 cloves garlic

1 teaspoon ground cumin

1. In a large skillet over medium heat, warm the oil. Cook the spinach, stirring frequently, for 5 minutes, or until wilted and tender.

2. In a blender, combine the spinach, broth, avocado, garlic, and cumin. Blend until the desired consistency is reached.

3. Transfer the blended soup to a stockpot over low heat and warm before serving.

Per serving: 133 calories, 12 g fat (2 g saturated fat), 6 g carbohydrates, 1 g sugar, 76 mg sodium, 3 g fiber, 1 g protein

MEDITERRANEAN ASPARAGUS SOUP

MAKES 4 SERVINGS

Asparagus may help our brains fight cognitive decline. It provides folate, which works with vitamin B_{12} to help prevent cognitive damage. In a study from Tufts University, older adults with healthy levels of folate and B_{12} performed better on a test of response speed and mental flexibility. This creamy soup is topped with feta cheese, a good source of vitamin B_{12}, which also promotes red blood cell production and keeps your brain sharp.

12 spears asparagus, woody ends trimmed and spears cut into 1" pieces

2 tablespoons extra virgin olive oil

1 medium sweet onion, sliced

2 cups low-sodium vegetable broth

$\frac{1}{2}$ cup tahini + 2 tablespoons for drizzling

$\frac{1}{4}$ cup finely chopped parsley

1 teaspoon minced garlic

1 cup unsweetened coconut milk

$\frac{1}{2}$ cup crumbled feta cheese

1. In a steamer over high heat, steam the asparagus for 8 minutes, or until soft.

2. In a large skillet over medium-high heat, warm the oil. Cook the onion, stirring frequently, for 7 minutes, or until golden brown.

3. In a blender, combine the asparagus, onion, broth, $\frac{1}{2}$ cup tahini, parsley, and garlic. Blend until the mixture reaches a chunky consistency.

4. Pour the mixture back into the skillet over low heat. Stir in the coconut milk. Heat through.

5. Drizzle the soup with the remaining 2 tablespoons tahini sauce and sprinkle it with the feta cheese before serving.

Per serving: 450 calories, 39 g fat (17 g saturated fat), 19 g carbohydrates, 6 g sugar, 307 mg sodium, 4 g fiber, 11 g protein

GENIUS-LEVEL GAZPACHO

MAKES 4 SERVINGS

This cooling, summery soup combines tomatoes, which are rich in lycopene, and cucumbers, which contain an antioxidant called fisetin that improves memory. Olive oil is the connective superstar here, as it's a great source of vitamin E, which minimizes cognitive decline, and is also rich in polyphenols, a group of chemicals with antioxidant and anti-inflammatory properties. Consuming polyphenols may inhibit the onset of Alzheimer's disease by preventing oxidative damage.

6 medium heirloom tomatoes (about 3 pounds), chopped

1 English cucumber, chopped (seeding and peeling are optional)

½ cup extra virgin olive oil + additional for drizzling

¼ cup balsamic vinegar

4 cloves garlic, smashed

Salt and ground black pepper

1 avocado, finely chopped

1. In a blender, puree the tomatoes and cucumbers. (If your blender is not large enough to blend all of the vegetables at once, you can blend them in 2 batches.)

2. Add the oil, vinegar, garlic, and salt and pepper to taste. Puree until the desired consistency is reached.

3. Refrigerate for a few hours. Serve cold, garnished with a drizzle of oil and the chopped avocado.

Per serving: 398 calories, 34 g fat (5 g saturated fat), 22 g carbohydrates, 12 g sugar, 265 mg sodium, 7 g fiber, 4 g protein

TOTAL RECALL
BROCCOLI SOUP

MAKES 4 SERVINGS

This unique combo blends the sweetness of coconut milk with mild-tasting broccoli, a star brain-boosting veggie. Broccoli contains high levels of vitamin K and choline, which strengthen your cognitive abilities and help keep your memory sharp.

1 tablespoon olive oil

1 yellow onion, chopped

2 cloves garlic, minced

1 tablespoon ground allspice

1 head broccoli, chopped

1 can (13.5 ounces) light coconut milk

1 cup low-sodium vegetable broth

1. In a large skillet over medium heat, warm the oil. Cook the onions, stirring frequently, for 7 minutes, or until soft and golden. Add the garlic and allspice and cook, stirring, for 3 minutes.

2. Add the broccoli, stirring to coat with the onion mixture. Pour the milk and broth over the broccoli. Simmer, covered, for 20 minutes, or until the broccoli is very tender.

3. Let the soup cool slightly before transferring it to a blender. Puree in batches until the desired consistency is reached. Reheat before serving.

Per serving: 148 calories, 11 g fat (6 g saturated fat), 11 g carbohydrates, 3 g sugar, 77 mg sodium, 3 g fiber, 4 g protein

CURRIED CARROT & SQUASH SOUP

MAKES 4 SERVINGS

This spicy puree includes a delicious fermented staple: kefir. Cultured foods like kefir, raw milk, and yogurt contain probiotics, which help promote healthy gut microbiota. A healthy gut has been shown to raise mood and help with anxiety and depression. Now that's a happy spoonful!

1 tablespoon olive oil

1 yellow onion, sliced

3 cups low-sodium vegetable broth

1 cup cooked baby carrots

1 cup canned sweet potatoes, drained

1 cup broiled yellow squash pieces

1 cup plain unsweetened kefir or plain 2% Greek yogurt

Juice of 2 limes

2 tablespoons grated fresh ginger

1 tablespoon curry powder

1 tablespoon ground turmeric

2 teaspoons rice vinegar

Salt and ground black pepper

¼ cup chopped fresh cilantro, for garnish

1. In a large saucepan over medium heat, warm the oil. Cook the onion for 7 minutes, or until transparent.

2. Add the broth, carrots, sweet potatoes, squash, kefir or Greek yogurt, lime juice, ginger, curry powder, turmeric, vinegar, and salt and pepper to taste. Bring to a boil, reduce heat to a simmer, and cook, uncovered, for about 15 minutes.

3. Remove from the heat and let the soup cool slightly. In a blender, puree the soup in batches, or use an immersion blender.

4. Pour the soup back into the pot and heat through. Garnish with the cilantro before serving.

Per serving: 178 calories, 6 g fat (2 g saturated fat), 26 g carbohydrates, 10 g sugar, 423 mg sodium, 4 g fiber, 5 g protein

Chapter

5

Heart Smarts

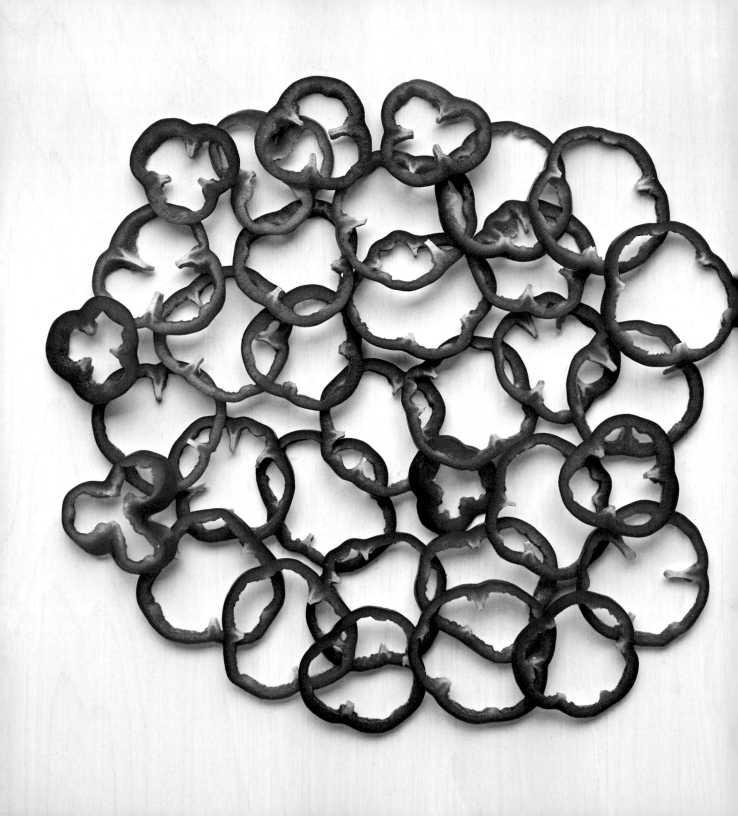

Dodge the № 1 Killer

The reasons to pay attention to heart health are stronger than ever: According to the Centers for Disease Control, 610,000 people die of heart disease in the United States every year—that's one in every four deaths. Fortunately, according to the American Heart Association, with diet and lifestyle changes, many women can reduce their chances of heart disease by nearly 80 percent! Hey, we know you're busy, but eating convenience foods will only add to the stress. It's never too early to start taking care of your heart through a balanced, uber-healthy diet.

MAKE SURE THE BEAT GOES ON

Most people who have atherosclerosis, coronary heart disease, high blood pressure, high cholesterol, and high triglycerides have no signs or symptoms. They may not be diagnosed with these medical issues until *after* a heart attack or stroke. *I'm not old*, you might be thinking, but it's more important than ever to keep your heart healthy from a young age. Don't wait until it is too late. As women, we focus on our OB/GYN checkups and mammograms, but too often we neglect our heart health. In addition to eating a healthy diet, remember to get yearly blood work, know your cholesterol numbers, get your blood pressure checked, cut back on high-cholesterol foods, and most importantly, take the time to put yourself first!

The Triglyceride Trap

Triglycerides are a type of fat in your blood that your body uses to produce energy. Sounds good, right? The problem is that when our triglyceride level gets too high, it increases our risk for heart disease. That's because high triglycerides can thicken the artery wall, which may cause a heart attack or stroke. By consuming too many starchy or sugary foods like pasta or sweets, you can raise your triglycerides to an unhealthy level. The right diet, however, can actually help keep them in check—and keep your ticker healthy for years to come. The

HOW TO LOWER YOUR TRIGLYCERIDES

- Limit fat and sugar intake.
- Maintain a healthy weight.
- Exercise five times per week for at least 30 minutes each time.
- Quit smoking.
- Reduce your alcohol consumption. (According to the Dietary Guidelines for Americans, moderate alcohol consumption is defined as having up to 1 drink per day for women and up to 2 drinks per day for men.)

soups and smoothies in this chapter are specifically designed to help keep your triglycerides under control.

The Truth about High Blood Pressure

When you think of a person with high blood pressure (HBP), you might imagine someone who is overworked, grouchy, or downright nasty. The truth is, high blood pressure, or hypertension, has nothing to do with a person's mood, temper, or personality. Calm people can also have elevated blood pressure. According to the National Heart, Lung, and Blood Institute, one in three US adults suffers from hypertension. That's approximately 72 million people! The good news is that a better diet can lower HBP and save your life!

To put it simply, blood pressure is the force with which blood moves through your arteries and veins. The more forcefully your heart pumps that blood, the more the arteries stretch to allow blood to flow. Over time, if the force of the bloodflow is constantly high, the walls of the arteries get overstretched and damaged. This creates problems in several ways.

- The overstretching creates weak areas in the blood vessels, making them more prone to rupture. Strokes and aneurysms are caused by ruptures in the blood vessels.

- The overstretching often causes tiny tears in the blood vessels that create scar tissue on the walls of arteries and veins. These tears and this scar tissue collect plaque deposits.

- Cholesterol and plaque buildup in the damaged arteries cause the bloodflow to become restricted or cut off. Thus, pressure is increased throughout your body, forcing the heart to work harder. If plaque breaks off or the buildup blocks the vessel, heart attacks and strokes occur.

High blood pressure can damage your heart, brain, eyes, and kidneys before you feel anything. So how does it happen? Our blood pressure elevates because of genetics or lifestyle factors, especially diet. Eating too many salty or processed foods, for example, can cause hypertension. Drinking too much alcohol and smoking also play huge

HEALTHY HEART SUPERSTARS

• Almonds are very high in monounsaturated fats, vitamin E, fiber, and protein. Walnuts are an excellent source of alpha-linolenic acid (ALA), which improves blood pressure and reduces inflammation.

• Asparagus is one of the best vegetables for clearing the arteries, as it's high in fiber and minerals, as well as vitamins C, E, K, B$_1$, and B$_2$. Asparagus lowers blood pressure and prevents blood clots.

• Avocado improves cholesterol by decreasing triglycerides and "bad" LDL cholesterol and increasing "good" HDL cholesterol. HDL cholesterol removes the LDL cholesterol and helps to keep your blood vessels free of plaque buildup.

• Broccoli is high in vitamin K, which prevents hardening of the arteries. Broccoli prevents oxidation of LDL cholesterol because it is loaded with antioxidants. The fiber in broccoli supports normal blood pressure and decreases the stress that causes tears in the artery walls.

• Chia seeds contain fiber and ALA, which keep arteries clear by regulating blood pressure, decreasing LDL cholesterol, lowering triglycerides, and raising HDL cholesterol.

• Cranberries are high in anti-oxidants that improve heart health by lowering LDL and increasing HDL cholesterol levels.

• Flaxseeds are high in ALA, which prevents and treats diseases of the heart and blood vessels. It can prevent heart attacks and lower high blood pressure.

• Persimmons are loaded with antioxidants and polyphenols, which decrease LDL and triglycerides. Persimmons are also high in fiber, which regulates blood pressure, keeps your heart healthy, and keeps your arteries free of plaque.

• Pomegranates have antioxidants that protect the circulatory system from plaque buildup and blood clots. Pomegranate stimulates nitric oxide production in the blood, which opens arteries and normalizes blood pressure.

• Turmeric's main component, curcumin, is a potent anti-inflammatory. Studies have shown that the high levels of curcumin in turmeric can aid in the reduction of fatty deposits in the arteries.

• Watermelon is an excellent source of the amino acid L-citrulline and keeps arteries clear by reducing blood pressure and diminishing inflammation.

• Whole grains such as quinoa, barley, and oats improve blood cholesterol levels due to their soluble fiber content.

roles in blood pressure. So, how do you lower HBP? If you have high blood pressure, we've handpicked some soups and smoothies in this chapter that should help.

Cholesterol Explained

Cholesterol is something your grandma worries about—not you. Well, actually, it is something you probably want to pay attention to, and it's not all bad. Your body needs it to make hormones, vitamin D, and substances that help you digest foods. There are two types of cholesterol: low-density lipoprotein (LDL) and high-density lipoprotein (HDL). LDL is known as "bad" cholesterol because it contributes to the plaque buildup that clogs arteries, which can lead to coronary artery disease and cardiovascular disease. That's why we need HDL, the "good" cholesterol, because it removes LDL from the arteries. Having high HDL protects against heart attack and stroke. See "Healthy Heart Superstars" for foods that lower LDL and increase HDL for overall better health.

Did you know?

Not only do they add flavor and warmth to any meal, but garlic and onions keep the blood to a consistency that can easily flow through arteries and veins. Their high sulfur content prevents calcium deposits and reduces the plaque that clogs the blood pathways of the body.

Fun facts about ...
PERSIMMONS

A Worldly Fruit

Persimmons are a lesser-known, exotic orange fruit that originated in China but have since spread across the globe, evolving into different varieties, from the Japanese persimmon to the American to the Indian and beyond. Persimmons belong to the *Diospyros* family, a genus of more than 700 types of trees and small shrubs that grow all over the world. They are both eaten plain and incorporated into many ethnic dishes. The shapes and colors of persimmons can vary quite a bit, but the taste remains pretty much the same across varieties: delicious!

THE ULTIMATE DETOX

We know you hear about detoxing all the time, but restricting your diet or "cleansing" with wacky juices isn't always the smartest plan. The best and easiest way to get rid of toxins in your body is to eat more fresh, whole foods—and persimmons are a great addition to a clean diet.

CLEAN UP YOUR HEALTH

Persimmons are an international delight that has been nicknamed "nature's candy" and "the fruit of the gods." But persimmons are much more than a tasty treat. They also have incredible health benefits.

HELP YOUR HEART

Let's talk about how persimmons do wonders for your heart. They have a significant amount of potassium, which lowers blood pressure by increasing bloodflow, keeping your cardiovascular system in top shape. Persimmons also contain copper, which helps create new red blood cells and keeps your blood circulating like it should. The more healthy red blood cells you have, the greater your energy, the higher your metabolism, and the better your brain function.

DEFY AGING

We love fruits packed with antioxidants, and persimmons top our list. If you want to keep a youthful glow—who doesn't?—persimmons are full of beta-carotene, vitamin A, and lutein, all of which help prevent signs of aging such as age spots and wrinkles.

PREVENT CANCER

Let's face it, the word *cancer* is scary. No one wants to be diagnosed with a painful illness, which is why we should incorporate more cancer-fighting foods into our diet as soon and as much as possible. Persimmons are cancer destroyers. Rich in antioxidants and vitamins C and A, they kick free radicals to the curb. A food that tastes as delicious as it is healthy? Yes, please!

Eat It Three Ways

Try persimmons fresh, dried, or cooked to experience their versatile flavor! Check out our I Heart Coconut Smoothie on page 121, perfect in late fall or early winter when American persimmons are in season.

CHOCOLATE BERRY SMOOTHIE

Science suggests the pigments that make up the red color in strawberries are powerful antioxidants that may reduce inflammation related to hardening of the arteries and decrease risk factors for heart disease. Cacao contains flavonoids, which are naturally occurring compounds in plants and have a protective effect on cardiovascular health. They can help prevent the oxidation of LDL cholesterol, which leads to the development of atherosclerotic plaque. They also regulate the constriction of blood vessels, prevent high blood pressure, and inhibit blood clots. All that in a blend of creamy goodness!

1 cup frozen strawberries

1 cup unsweetened almond milk or coconut milk

½ cup plain 2% Greek yogurt

2 tablespoons cacao nibs*

1 tablespoon unsweetened cocoa powder

In a blender, combine the strawberries, almond or coconut milk, yogurt, cacao nibs, and cocoa powder. Blend until the desired consistency is reached.

Per serving: 260 calories, 12 g fat (4 g saturated fat), 30 g carbohydrates, 13 g sugar, 237 mg sodium, 10 g fiber, 13 g protein

❋ For extra flavor (and heart health benefits), sprinkle extra cacao nibs on top of the smoothie as a garnish.

STRAWBERRY SWOON SMOOTHIE

This tropical blend combines orange juice, which can help improve bloodflow, and potassium-rich banana and papaya. According to the National Academy of Sciences, a diet rich in potassium may decrease your risk of high blood pressure and stroke.

1 cup orange juice (from 2–4 medium oranges)

1 cup fresh or frozen strawberries

1 cup chopped fresh or frozen papaya

1 banana

¼ cup lemon juice (from 1 large lemon)

Several ice cubes

In a blender, combine the orange juice, strawberries, papaya, banana, lemon juice, and ice cubes. Blend until the desired consistency is reached.

Per serving: 338 calories, 2 g fat (0.5 g saturated fat), 84 g carbohydrates, 55 g sugar, 19 mg sodium, 9 g fiber, 5 g protein

I HEART COCONUT SMOOTHIE

Fans of coconut rejoice! The fat in coconut oil (in moderation) can boost your HDL or "good" cholesterol. You'll keep the beat going with this creamy blend of heart-healthy ingredients.

2 medium persimmons, stemmed and peeled

1 cup unsweetened coconut milk or cashew milk

1 tablespoon ground flaxseeds

1 teaspoon lemon juice

$\frac{1}{2}$ teaspoon ground cinnamon

$\frac{1}{2}$ teaspoon vanilla extract

In a blender, combine the persimmons, coconut or cashew milk, flaxseeds, lemon juice, cinnamon, and vanilla. Blend until the desired consistency is reached.

Per serving: 161 calories, 8 g fat (5 g saturated fat), 21 g carbohydrates, 1 g sugar, 18 mg sodium, 3 g fiber, 3 g protein

TAKE MY PULSE SMOOTHIE

MAKES 1 SERVING

Watermelon is one of the richest sources of the amino acid citrulline, which opens veins and arteries to improve bloodflow and reduce blood pressure. That helps keep arteries clear and leads to improved circulation and overall cardiovascular health. This summery smoothie also blends in chia seeds—an excellent source of omega-3 fatty acids, which help to raise HDL ("good") cholesterol levels.

2 cups watermelon chunks

1 cup frozen strawberries

1 tablespoon chia seeds

1 tablespoon lime juice

2 teaspoons agave nectar, or to taste

In a blender, combine the watermelon, strawberries, chia seeds, lime juice, and agave nectar. Blend until the desired consistency is reached.

Per serving: 241 calories, 4 g fat (0.5 g saturated fat), 53 g carbohydrates, 35 g sugar, 9 mg sodium, 8 g fiber, 4 g protein

Did you know?

Antioxidants in strawberries lower LDL ("bad") cholesterol, and their high potassium helps manage blood pressure. Strawberries also contain folate, which helps maintain normal blood levels of an amino acid called homocysteine that, when out of control, can contribute to a higher risk of heart disease.

CRUNCHY CRANBERRY-POM SMOOTHIE BOWL

MAKES 2 SERVINGS

Cranberries are packed with antioxidant power that lowers bad cholesterol to protect your heart and improve your health. Layer up this smoothie bowl for a satisfying breakfast or any-time-of-the-day treat!

1 cup frozen cranberries

1 cup pomegranate juice

$\frac{1}{2}$ cup rolled (old-fashioned) oats

6 ounces ($\frac{2}{3}$–$\frac{3}{4}$ cup) low-fat plain, vanilla, or berry yogurt

In a blender, combine the cranberries, pomegranate juice, oats, and yogurt. Blend until a thick consistency is reached. Pour the smoothie into a bowl and sprinkle it with your desired toppings.

Per serving: 648 calories, 22 g fat (4 g saturated fat), 98 g carbohydrates, 54 g sugar, 147 mg sodium, 15 g fiber, 22 g protein

TOPPINGS

$\frac{1}{4}$ cup chopped or slivered almonds

$\frac{1}{4}$ cup blueberries, blackberries, boysenberries, and/or raspberries

1 tablespoon flaxseeds or chia seeds

Did you know?

Some nuts contain plant sterols, substances that lower cholesterol. Nuts are also high in omega-3 fatty acids, which prevent irregular heart rhythms that lead to heart attacks, and they're a source of L-arginine, a substance that makes arteries more flexible and less susceptible to blood clots that block bloodflow. Almonds in particular are high in healthy fats and vitamin E—so next time you're looking for a quick and healthy snack, grab a handful!

CINNAMON OAT HEALTHY HEART SMOOTHIE

MAKES 1 SERVING

Bananas contain potassium, critical for heart health, and oats provide soluble and insoluble fiber to lower cholesterol levels. Cinnamon has also been linked to a reduced risk of heart disease. We "heart" this yummy combo as the perfect break-fast treat.

2 frozen bananas

¼ cup rolled (old-fashioned) oats

1 cup unsweetened vanilla or plain almond milk

¼ teaspoon ground cinnamon

1 teaspoon honey

In a blender, combine the bananas, oats, almond milk, cinnamon, and honey. Blend until the desired consistency is reached and enjoy!

Per serving: 348 calories, 5 g fat (0.5 g saturated fat), 76 g carbohydrates, 35 g sugar, 183 mg sodium, 10 g fiber, 6 g protein

Did you know?

If your potassium levels are too high or too low, you may be at increased risk of a cardiac arrest. Potassium-rich foods help keep your heart beating regularly, and they can also help lower your blood pressure.

ASPARAGUS & BROCCOLI SOUP

MAKES 4 SERVINGS

Asparagus is one of the best vegetables for clearing arteries, as it's full of fiber and minerals as well as vitamins C, E, K, B$_1$, and B$_2$. Asparagus can also help lower blood pressure and prevent blood clots. Broccoli is high in vitamin K, which helps prevent hardening of the arteries. Combined, they pack a one-two punch against heart disease.

2 tablespoons extra virgin olive oil

1 pound asparagus, trimmed and chopped

2 cups broccoli florets

¼ cup chopped yellow onions

2 tablespoons minced garlic

5 cups low-sodium vegetable broth

1 cup unsweetened almond milk or cashew milk

½ teaspoon salt

½ teaspoon ground white pepper

Grated Parmesan cheese (optional)

1. In a stockpot over medium-high heat, warm the oil. Add the asparagus, broccoli, onions, and garlic. Cook for about 5 minutes, or until the onions are softened.

2. Add the broth and bring to a boil, lower the heat, and simmer, uncovered, for about 15 minutes, or until the vegetables are soft. Remove from the heat and cool slightly.

3. Working in batches, puree the soup in a blender until smooth. Add the almond or cashew milk in one of the batches.

4. Pour the soup back into the pot, add the salt and pepper, and heat through. Serve sprinkled with a pinch of Parmesan, if desired.

Per serving: 173 calories, 12 g fat (2 g saturated fat), 13 g carbohydrates, 4 g sugar, 524 mg sodium, 5 g fiber, 4 g protein

CREAMY SWEET POTATO SOUP

Research in the *British Journal of Nutrition* has found that eating more deep orange–colored fruits and vegetables like carrots and sweet potatoes is associated with a lower risk of coronary heart disease. Credit high levels of beta-carotene, the compound responsible for both the bright hue and heart-healthy attributes. Sweet potatoes have the added benefit of being high in magnesium, which supports healthy artery, blood, heart, and nerve function. Serve up this creamy and delicious soup and your heart will thank you.

1 tablespoon olive oil

1 medium onion, chopped

½ clove garlic, minced

2 cups water

1 cup low-sodium chicken broth

4 large carrots, chopped

1 medium sweet potato, peeled and finely chopped

1 red bell pepper, seeded and chopped

1 tablespoon chopped fresh ginger

¼ cup plain 2% Greek yogurt

Chopped fresh cilantro (optional)

1. In a large saucepan over medium-high heat, warm the oil. Cook the onion and garlic, stirring frequently, for 2 to 3 minutes, or until the onion is tender. Add the water and broth. Bring to a boil.

2. Add the carrots, sweet potato, bell pepper, and ginger. Reduce the heat and simmer, uncovered, for 15 minutes. Remove from the heat and cool slightly.

3. Working in batches, puree the soup in a blender until smooth.

4. Return the soup to the pan and cook over medium heat for 15 to 20 minutes, or until warmed through and thickened.

5. Stir in the yogurt and serve immediately, topped with cilantro, if desired.

Per serving: 129 calories, 4 g fat (1 g saturated fat), 20 g carbohydrates, 8 g sugar, 93 mg sodium, 4 g fiber, 4 g protein

CAULIFLOWER-KALE SOUP

MAKES 4 SERVINGS

Cauliflower is high in fiber and contains allicin, which lowers the risk of heart attacks and reduces cholesterol. It also contains vitamins K and C, antioxidants, and omega-3 fatty acids, which prevent plaque buildup, decreasing the chances of high blood pressure and high cholesterol. Kale is everywhere for a reason—this dark green wonder contains omega-3 fatty acids that control blood clotting and protect against heart disease and stroke. Kale also packs potassium, fiber, and vitamins B$_6$ and C, which support a healthy heart (and body too).

1 tablespoon extra virgin olive oil

1 medium onion, chopped

5 cups chopped kale

4 cups cauliflower florets

1 large potato, peeled and chopped

3 cloves garlic, minced

3½ cups low-sodium vegetable broth

½ cup plain unsweetened almond milk

Juice of 1 lemon

1. In a large pot over medium-high heat, warm the oil. Cook the onion, stirring frequently, for 5 minutes, or until translucent. Add the kale, cauliflower, potato, and garlic. Cook, stirring, for about 5 minutes.

2. Add the broth and bring the soup to a boil. Reduce the heat and simmer, uncovered, for 30 minutes, or until the cauliflower and potato are tender. Add the almond milk and lemon juice.

3. Let the soup cool slightly, then use an immersion blender to blend until smooth. Or use a standard blender, blending in batches if necessary.

4. Reheat before serving.

Per serving: 212 calories, 5 g fat (1 g saturated fat), 36 g carbohydrates, 5 g sugar, 215 mg sodium, 6 g fiber, 8 g protein

✳ Cauliflower may turn an unappetizing yellow, brown, or even blue-green color in alkaline water, which is often found in aluminum or iron cookware—the chemicals react with the cauliflower. You can add a tablespoon of lemon juice to the water to prevent this.

BLENDED ARTICHOKE & CARROT SOUP

Studies have shown a relationship between high-potassium diets and reduced risk of stroke—and artichokes contain large amounts of potassium, which helps regulate heart rhythm and maintain normal blood pressure. Certain phytonutrients in artichokes also decrease LDL cholesterol and reduce the overall risk of heart disease.

¼ cup olive oil

1 can (14 ounces) artichoke hearts, drained

1 cup baby carrots

½ cup chopped yellow onions

½ cup lemon juice

4 teaspoons chopped fresh dill, divided

2 cups low-sodium vegetable broth

1 tablespoon crushed garlic

1. In a large saucepan over medium-high heat, warm the oil. Add the artichoke hearts, carrots, onions, lemon juice, and 2 teaspoons of the dill. Cook, stirring frequently, for 5 minutes.

2. Add the broth. Bring to a boil, then lower the heat and simmer, covered, for 15 minutes, or until the vegetables are soft.

3. Let the soup cool slightly. Working in batches, transfer the soup to a blender. Add the garlic and blend until smooth.

4. Return the soup to the pan and reheat thoroughly before serving garnished with the remaining 2 teaspoons of dill.

Per serving: 186 calories, 14 g fat (2 g saturated fat), 14 g carbohydrates, 5 g sugar, 278 mg sodium, 2 g fiber, 2 g protein

HEART-STRONG SPINACH SOUP

Popeye was right—spinach is a powerful food! High in vitamin C, beta-carotene, and other nutrients that prevent cholesterol buildup in the blood vessel walls, spinach also contains folate, which lowers blood levels of the amino acid homocysteine, associated with heart disease and stroke. The potassium and magnesium in spinach lower blood pressure and the risk of cardiovascular disease.

4–5 cups chopped spinach

2 cups water

1 cup chopped fresh basil

1 small cucumber, peeled and chopped

¼ cup chopped red onion

¼ cup almonds, cashews, or pine nuts

2 tablespoons olive oil

1 clove garlic

1 vine-ripened tomato, chopped, for garnish

½ cup chopped avocado, for garnish

In a blender, combine the spinach, water, basil, cucumber, onion, nuts, oil, and garlic. Blend until the desired consistency is reached. Serve cold, garnished with the tomato and avocado.

Per serving: 172 calories, 15 g fat (2 g saturated fat), 8 g carbohydrates, 2 g sugar, 23 mg sodium, 4 g fiber, 4 g protein

✳ Cashews, which are used as a substitute for milk, cream, and cheese in vegan diets, have a high fat content; therefore, if they are kept at room temperature, they will not stay fresh. Store them in an airtight container in the refrigerator and they will last 4 to 6 months. You can also freeze them for up to 8 months.

Chapter

6

Hormone Happiness

Conquer Cravings and Ward Off Infections

Women's Health isn't just the name of our magazine— it's our absolute passion. Every day, we're scouring the latest studies in science and medical journals so you'll have as much information as possible when making decisions about your body and what's best for you. Many times, those decisions go hand-in-hand with being a woman: what to do about PMS, how to avoid urinary tract infections (UTIs), whether there are ways to make menopause more bearable, and how to safeguard your fertility, even if you already have kids or aren't sure you want them. What you eat can play a surprisingly big role in addressing those issues and more, which is why we've come up with recipes specifically designed to do just that.

COMMON HEALTH CONCERNS FOR WOMEN

Here's the deal: Despite how freakin' awesome it is to be a woman, some of the things that make us unique can also make us feel, well, less than awesome. And while we absolutely celebrate normalizing things like having your period, these totally normal bodily functions can often slow us down. The good news is that there are more ways than ever to get the right nutritional balance to stay healthy no matter what time of the month it is. In this chapter, we compiled the most common women's health issues and created simple, delicious recipes and nutritional tips to combat them.

Power Up Your Period

Periods come with a boatload of less-than-ideal symptoms from cramps to PMS to bloating. Through eating the right foods, you can avoid the negative aspects of menstruation. For example, when it comes to PMS, calcium is your best friend. According to a joint study by researchers from the University of Massachusetts at Amherst and other institutions, which analyzed the calcium and vitamin D intakes of approximately 3,000 women, consuming a diet with calcium-rich dairy products—especially those with added vitamin D—lowered the risk for developing PMS by as much as 40 percent! So if cramps, bloating, and irritability have you down, try eating more of the following:

- **PEANUTS AND PEANUT BUTTER** are high in vitamin B_6 and magnesium. Magnesium controls serotonin, the "feel-good chemical" that helps combat depression. Extra magnesium will improve your mood. Bonus: It minimizes bloating.

- **BROCCOLI** contains vitamins A, B_6, C, and E and the minerals calcium, potassium, and magnesium, which also whup PMS symptoms.

- **BANANAS** are rich in B_6 and in potassium, which prevents water retention and bloating and relieves cramping.

- **OATS** are one of the top foods for women who suffer from painful menstrual cycles since they are high in zinc and magnesium, which are cramp-fighting vitamins and minerals.

- **SPINACH AND KALE** are high in calcium, which alleviates menstrual cramps. They also contain high amounts of vitamins B_6 and E and magnesium, which ward off nausea and stomach pains.

- **PUMPKIN AND SUNFLOWER SEEDS** contain the "menstruation cramp relief vitamin," vitamin E. They also have zinc, which minimizes bloating and pain during our cycles. Sunflower seeds are an excellent source of vitamin B_6, which supports zinc and magnesium absorption, thus assisting in pain relief.

- **SESAME SEEDS** contain healthy fatty acids that relax stomach muscles and decrease cramping. These seeds are rich in vitamin B_6, calcium, and magnesium—all PMS-easers.

Keep Bacteria at Bay

Oh, the joy of UTIs. If you're lucky enough not to have experienced one, they're bacterial infections that make it super uncomfortable—often painful—to use the bathroom. One in two women will get a UTI in her lifetime, and many of those women will have recurring infections. One of the main causes is *E. coli* bacteria. This is why it's important to wipe from front to back after using the bathroom. The urethra, the tube that moves urine from the bladder to the exterior of the body, is positioned close to the anus, and bacteria from the large intestine, such as *E. coli*, are in the ideal spot to escape the anus and infect the urethra. The bacteria travel up to the bladder and on to infect the kidneys. That's why it is so crucial to treat a UTI as soon as symptoms arise. In addition, sex can also transport bacteria into the urinary tract. But just know that UTIs are normal among women. It's hard not to feel embarrassed if you are diagnosed with this pesky infection, but the truth is, they're very common. Here are the top three foods that help prevent UTIs. All are easily incorporated into recipes like the Comforting Cranberry Smoothie (page 152), or even added to your diet.

- **CRANBERRIES** contain compounds that inhibit the bacteria that infect our urinary tract. (Tip: Try to avoid cranberry juice from concentrate as it's full of sugar and has way less of the good nutrients found in whole cranberries or pure cranberry juice.)

- **PINEAPPLE** contains an enzyme called bromelain, which reduces inflammation from infection and can help minimize the pain and discomfort that accompany a UTI.

- **PROBIOTICS** are healthy bacteria that strengthen your immune system and help fight infection. Think yogurt with live cultures, which is loaded with probiotics. Don't eat dairy? Try yogurt made from coconut, soy, or almond milk, but make sure it still has the live active cultures.

Keep Hormones in Check

As women, our hormone production works a little differently than men's—we have more estrogen and less testosterone, and sometimes what we eat can affect our hormones or even throw them off. The key is to balance your diet, since some foods aggravate your natural hormone production. For example, some foods like soy contain elements that mimic the activity of estrogen, so eating too much—or too little—can cause hormonal imbalances. If you're experiencing an imbalance or overload of estrogen, try eating foods with phytoestrogens, which boost estrogen levels and can prevent or ease symptoms. It'll keep your menstruation normal and your emotions in check!

Symptoms of high estrogen

Bloating
Swelling and tenderness in the breasts
Irregular menstrual periods
Headaches
Mood swings
Fibrocystic developments in the breast
Weight gain
Hair loss
Cold hands or feet
Fatigue
Difficulty remembering things
Trouble sleeping
Increased symptoms of PMS

Symptoms of low estrogen

Hot flashes

Night sweats

Anxiety

Vaginal dryness

Loss of libido

Mood swings

Depression

Panic attacks

Low self-esteem

Memory lapses

Phytoestrogens

Apples

Bell peppers

Broccoli

Brussels sprouts

Cabbage

Carrots

Cauliflower

Cherries

Chile peppers

Cranberries

Eggplant

Tomatoes

Garlic

Olives

Onions

Pomegranates

Potatoes

Yams

Feed Your Fertility

According to the Centers for Disease Control and Prevention, 7.4 million women have received treatment for infertility in the United States, and 1 in 8 couples have trouble getting pregnant. Fertility issues can be caused by many different things, from age and genetics to obesity and poor health. One of the most important things you can do whether you are trying to conceive or are already pregnant is to take great care of your body by eating a healthy, balanced, nutrient-rich diet. To keep your reproductive system in tip-top shape, we recommend eating a healthy dose of the following:

DAIRY is rich in calcium, a nutrient that is critical for reproductive health. Consume daily servings of milk, yogurt, leafy greens, tofu, almonds, and fortified juices. When you get pregnant, calcium is required for the development of your baby's bones and teeth.

IRON is a critical nutrient that helps

increase fertility. Studies show that women who increase iron intake during the preconception period have a higher fertility rate than women who are iron-deficient. In addition to iron-rich lean animal protein, there are many plant foods high in iron such as spinach, sweet potatoes, peas, broccoli, beet greens, collards, kale, and chard.

OMEGA-3 FATTY ACIDS found in fish such as salmon and sardines also boost fertility. They regulate reproductive hormones and increase bloodflow to reproductive organs. Other great sources of omega-3 fatty acids include flaxseeds, pumpkin seeds, and walnuts.

ZINC is important for getting pregnant. Zinc deficiency slows the production of high-quality eggs. Zinc-rich foods include beef, dairy, poultry, nuts, eggs, whole grains, and legumes.

FOLIC ACID should be in your system before you get pregnant, since it is one of the critical building blocks for a healthy baby. It is recommended to take folic acid up to 3 months prior to getting pregnant. Consuming foods high in folic acid is also important. Excellent sources include beans, peas, spinach, collard greens, kale, turnip greens, broccoli, asparagus, and citrus fruits.

Tip: Your health affects your baby's health. When you decide to quit smoking and drinking, remind yourself every day why you are making these changes. Do not keep alcohol or cigarettes at home, avoid places that tempt you to drink or smoke (like clubs or casinos), and educate yourself about what drinking and smoking do to your child while you are pregnant.

Help, I'm Gonna Hurl . . .

Whether you are pregnant and in the throes of morning sickness (which, frankly, should be called "all-day sickness") or experiencing queasiness due to a hormonal imbalance or emotional distress, many women suffer from debilitating nausea and/or stomachaches. As women, we do so much that our mental stress can sometimes take a toll on our physical state! Here are some specific foods that help fight the symptoms of nausea and soothe your stomach. You can also try blending the Easy, Not Queasy Ginger Smoothie on page 151 for a more even-keeled start to your day.

GINGER acts as an antiseptic and helps alleviate nausea.

BANANAS replenish potassium in the body lost due to vomiting.

PEACHES are a good source of fiber and help soothe the stomach.

Tip: There are a lot of wacky solutions to combat morning sickness, but as long as they're nontoxic, we're willing to try! Some believe that eating a cold meal rather than a hot one can help with morning sickness. Also, it has been said that sniffing lemons helps alleviate nausea. Some women find their own specific practices to help. We're all for it! Just make sure it is safe.

Fun facts about ...
PUMPKINS

A Seasonal Sensation

When you think of pumpkin, what's the first thing that comes to mind? Jack-o'-lanterns? Thanksgiving? Pie? Once the weather gets crisp and cool, we go nuts for the orange gourd—from pumpkin spice lattes to pies to muffins and more. But pumpkin is much more than a Halloween decoration or a flavor to jazz up your coffee (though we love that too!). The health benefits of pumpkins are huge, especially for women. Whether you buy it canned (hint: make sure it's BPA free!), make your own puree, or bake the seeds, you should definitely add more pumpkin to your diet.

CYCLE SAVER

Pumpkin and pumpkin seeds ease cramps and bloating. According to the University of Maryland Medical Center, they can help reduce pain during menstruation because they're full of vitamin E. When you know your cycle is around the corner, try the Pumpkin Spice Smoothie on page 148.

POSTMENOPAUSE HEALTH PROMOTER

Is your period a thing of the past? Or are you in perimenopause, the stage where your body prepares itself for menopause? Symptoms typically start when you are in your forties or early fifties; however, it's possible to go through perimenopause in your early thirties!

Either way, pumpkin is a good food for you. In fact, the oil in pumpkin seeds has phytoestrogens, which, according to the US National Library of Medicine, help with menopausal symptoms like hot flashes, joint pain, and headaches. Phytoestrogen also helps raise HDL, or "good" cholesterol, which can be very important when you pass the period years.

Beyond Women's Health

Pumpkins rock for our reproductive health, but they're actually just good for us, period—feel free to share the benefits with your significant other too. Here are some more reasons everyone should be noshing on more orange goodness.

FLU SEASON FRIEND

Fall is the start of cold and flu season, and it also happens to be when pumpkin grows best. Luckily, nature understands our needs, because pumpkin is perfect for strengthening your immune system. The zinc found in pumpkin seeds and sunflower seeds supports healthy immunity, and it also helps with sleep, mood, and eye and skin health. The Standard American Diet (or SAD) is pretty low in zinc, which can translate into chronic fatigue, acne, and even depression.

BRAIN HEALTH

When you think about omega-3 fatty acids, you might think of fish like salmon or even krill oil. But those of us who don't eat a lot of seafood need to get omega-3s somewhere else. It turns out pumpkin seeds are an amazing source of plant-based omega-3s. There are an insane amount of benefits of consuming omega-3s, from fighting depression to staving off memory loss. Plus, they taste great when baked with cinnamon or sea salt, depending on your flavor preference.

SWEET DREAMS

Sleep is critical for our overall health, but with busy schedules, on-screen distractions, and late nights, it's not easy to tuck in for a solid 6 to 8 hours every night. Pumpkin seeds are a natural sleep aid because they contain tryptophan (the same amino acid that makes us sleepy after a turkey dinner), which our bodies convert into melatonin, a hormone that helps control our sleep/wake cycles. If you're having trouble falling asleep, try a handful of pumpkin seeds.

BLOAT-BUSTING BANANA-ORANGE SMOOTHIE

MAKES 1 SERVING

This yummy combo is perfect as a pick-me-up on days when PMS has you down. The ginger helps relieve menstrual pain and cramps, and the oats are high in zinc and magnesium, which can also help prevent and ease cramps. Bananas are loaded with vitamin B_6, which lessens cramping, and high in potassium, which reduces water retention and bloating.

1½ cups unsweetened almond milk, coconut milk, or coconut water

1 orange, peeled

1 fresh or frozen banana

1 cup frozen strawberries

½ cup rolled (old-fashioned) oats

¼ teaspoon ground ginger

¼ teaspoon ground cinnamon

¼ teaspoon ground turmeric

In a blender, combine the milk or water, orange, banana, strawberries, oats, ginger, cinnamon, and turmeric. Blend until the desired consistency is reached.

Per serving: 441 calories, 8 g fat (1 g saturated fat), 89 g carbohydrates, 34 g sugar, 276 mg sodium, 15 g fiber, 10 g protein

✳ Drinking more water is the best way to beat the bloating that comes with PMS. Drinking water encourages your body to release the water that it is storing. Also, limit the amount of salt in your diet the week before your period to prevent water retention, and add fiber to your diet since fiber binds to estrogen, making it easier for us to eliminate the excess hormone.

PUMPKIN SPICE SMOOTHIE

MAKES 1 SERVING

In addition to the power-packed pumpkin in this smoothie, dates add potassium and magnesium, and cinnamon contains anti-inflammatory antioxidants, all of which can help relieve cramps, mood swings, and other symptoms of PMS. Whip up this smoothie as the perfect treat to get yourself back on track.

1 cup canned pumpkin puree

1 cup unsweetened almond milk or coconut milk

4 Medjool dates, pitted

2 tablespoons natural peanut butter or sunflower seed butter

¼ teaspoon ground cinnamon

¼ teaspoon ground nutmeg

In a blender, combine the pumpkin, milk, dates, peanut or sunflower seed butter, cinnamon, and nutmeg. Blend until the desired consistency is reached, and serve immediately.

Per serving: 294 calories, 20 g fat (2.5 g saturated fat), 102 g carbohydrates, 74 g sugar, 193 mg sodium, 17 g fiber, 12 g protein

✳ To make prep time easier, buy a large can of pumpkin puree and freeze 1-cup portions in zip-top bags to use as needed. The frozen puree will make the smoothie extra thick and creamy.

Did you know?

Pumpkin contains iron, which promotes fertility, according to Harvard Medical School's Harvard Health Publications. The vitamin A in pumpkin (consumed as beta-carotene, then converted to vitamin A in the body) is important for hormone synthesis during pregnancy and lactation.

CHOCOLATE-CRAVER'S SMOOTHIE

MAKES 2 SERVINGS

The hidden ingredient here is kale, which is high in calcium, vitamins B$_6$ and E, and magnesium, all of which help to relieve menstrual cramps. The raw cacao powder contains antioxidants and the minerals magnesium and iron that relieve PMS symptoms and make this smoothie taste like a decadent treat!

1 cup unsweetened almond milk

3 large leaves kale

1 frozen banana

2 tablespoons raw almonds

2 tablespoons unsweetened cacao powder

1 tablespoon sunflower seed butter

½" piece of fresh ginger, peeled

1 teaspoon agave nectar or honey

In a blender, combine the almond milk, kale, banana, almonds, cacao powder, sunflower seed butter, ginger, and agave nectar or honey to taste. Blend until the desired consistency is reached, then serve and enjoy!

Per serving: 532 calories, 28 g fat (5 g saturated fat), 61 g carbohydrates, 22 g sugar, 285 mg sodium, 17 g fiber, 19 g protein

Did you know?

Sunflower seeds (and sunflower seed butter) are high in vitamin E, zinc, and vitamin B$_6$, which decrease bloating and cravings and can assist in pain relief. Sprinkle a few into any smoothie for extra benefits.

EASY, NOT QUEASY GINGER SMOOTHIE

MAKES 1 SERVING

Ginger is an anti-inflammatory and can provide relief for nausea and pain. Peaches are a good source of fiber and soothe the stomach. Mix up this simple smoothie for a dose of soothing yet energizing goodness to get your day started right.

2 cups frozen peaches

¾ cup unsweetened coconut milk

1 tablespoon honey

2 teaspoons grated fresh ginger*

In a blender, combine the peaches, coconut milk, honey, and ginger. Blend until smooth. (You can add more or less coconut milk to reach your desired consistency.)

Per serving: 205 calories, 4 g fat (4 g saturated fat), 47 g carbohydrates, 41 g sugar, 13 mg sodium, 4 g fiber, 3 g protein

✳ When selecting fresh ginger, choose hearty, firm roots with a strong fragrance and smooth skin. The skin should not be cracked or withered. Ginger can be refrigerated in plastic wrap for up to 1 week. If you want to keep it longer than a week, peel the root and place it in a container of sherry before refrigerating it.

COMFORTING CRANBERRY SMOOTHIE

If you're suffering from a UTI, this smoothie is a natural Rx. Cranberries contain compounds that help prevent or ease the painful symptoms of a UTI. Pineapple contains an enzyme called bromelain, which decreases inflammation from infection, and the yogurt offers probiotics, or healthy bacteria that can help strengthen your immune system.

½ cup unsweetened cranberry juice

½ cup fresh or frozen cranberries

½ cup fresh, frozen, or canned pineapple chunks

½ cup blueberries

1 banana

6 ounces low-fat plain, vanilla, or berry yogurt

In a blender, combine the cranberry juice, cranberries, pineapple, blueberries, banana, and yogurt. Blend until the desired consistency is reached, adding more cranberry juice if necessary, then serve.

Per serving: 377 calories, 4 g fat (2 g saturated fat), 82 g carbohydrates, 59 g sugar, 125 mg sodium, 8 g fiber, 12 g protein

✻ If you don't eat dairy, try yogurt made from soy, almond, or coconut milk, but make sure it has the live active cultures.

CALMING GREEN SMOOTHIE

MAKES 1 SERVING

This smoothie is packed with fruits, veggies, and nutrient-rich seeds that combine to help you feel calm, cool, and collected. Spinach contains anti-inflammatory omega-3 fatty acids, and the kiwi and blueberries are high in vitamins C, E, and fiber. Blend up this baby for supergreen benefits.

1 cup spinach

1 cup unsweetened coconut milk, almond milk, or coconut water

$\frac{1}{2}$ cup low-fat plain yogurt

1 kiwifruit

$\frac{1}{2}$ avocado

$\frac{1}{4}$ cup fresh or frozen blueberries

1 tablespoon sesame seeds

1 tablespoon flaxseeds

In a blender, combine the spinach, milk or water, yogurt, kiwi, avocado, blueberries, and seeds, and blend until smooth. Drink immediately.

Per serving: 467 calories, 31 g fat (9.5 g saturated fat), 41 g carbohydrates, 13 g sugar, 130 mg sodium, 15 g fiber, 15 g protein

Did you know?

Sesame seeds are high in calcium and magnesium, which protect bone health, and they also contain tryptophan, an amino acid that manufactures mood-lifting serotonin and that our bodies convert into sleep-causing melatonin. Flaxseeds contain phytoestrogens that help control estrogen in your body and are a good source of vitamin B_6, which lifts your mood.

CHILLED CARROT & CAULIFLOWER SOUP

MAKES 4 SERVINGS

Cauliflower, onions, and carrots all contain phytoestrogens, which increase estrogen and prevent or ease menstrual and menopausal symptoms. Topped with a dollop of Greek yogurt, this delicious chilled soup is both satisfying *and* beneficial.

1 tablespoon olive oil

1 yellow onion, chopped

2 cups low-sodium vegetable broth

2 cups water

5 medium carrots, chopped

½ head cauliflower, cut into florets

1 teaspoon ground cumin

1 teaspoon ground coriander

1 cup plain 2% Greek yogurt, divided

Salt and ground black pepper

1. In a large saucepan over medium heat, warm the oil. Cook the onion, stirring frequently, for 5 minutes, or until soft.

2. Add the broth, water, carrots, cauliflower, cumin, and coriander, and bring to a boil. Reduce the heat, cover, and simmer for 30 minutes, or until the carrots are very tender.

3. Turn off the heat and let the soup cool slightly. Working in batches, add the soup to a blender and puree until smooth.

4. Pour the soup into a large bowl and whisk in ½ cup of the yogurt. Season to taste with salt and pepper. Cover and chill for at least 2 hours, or overnight.

5. Serve the soup with a dollop of the remaining ½ cup yogurt on top.

Per serving: 141 calories, 5 g fat (1.5 g saturated fat), 18 g carbohydrates, 9 g sugar, 238 mg sodium, 5 g fiber, 7 g protein

❋ You can do lots with Greek yogurt in addition to adding a dollop onto soups and smoothies! Yogurt is a natural meat tenderizer. Mix it with spices and use it on chicken or fish. It can also be mixed with honey or herbs and used as a creamy dressing.

Greek yogurt makes a lighter dip than sour cream, and the cooling effect of yogurt is a great way to balance the heat of curries and spicy dishes.

CHILLED MINT-MELON SOUP

MAKES 4 SERVINGS

This cooling soup blends specific fruits that offer relief when you're feeling queasy. Gingerroot contains chemicals called gingerols and shogaols that relieve nausea and vomiting. Watermelon eases heartburn and reduces swelling, due to its high water content and fruit sugars. It also alleviates morning sickness and dehydration. Coconut water is a terrific hydrator as it contains calcium, magnesium, potassium, and sodium.

6 cups canned coconut water

3 cups chopped watermelon

2 cups chopped cantaloupe

1 cup lemon juice

2" piece of fresh ginger, peeled and grated

6 mint leaves, halved lengthwise

1 teaspoon agave nectar, or to taste

In a large bowl, combine the coconut water, melons, lemon juice, ginger, mint leaves, and agave nectar. Blend until the desired consistency is reached. Serve chilled.

Per serving: 146 calories, 0 g fat (0 g saturated fat), 37 g carbohydrates, 31 g sugar, 80 mg sodium, 1 g fiber, 3 g protein

Did you know?

Lemons are acidic but, when digested, they raise your body's alkalinity, which restores its pH balance. This alkalinity action relieves the nausea that was due to imbalance in the gut.

HOT & FLASHY SOUP

MAKES 4 SERVINGS

Both Brussels sprouts and onions contain phytoestrogens, which can help boost estrogen levels and combat hot flashes. Whip up this confidence-boosting soup to soothe troublesome temperature changes and ease your way through perimeno-pausal symptoms.

1 tablespoon olive oil

1 cup finely chopped onion

¼ cup finely chopped red bell pepper

6 cloves garlic

5 cups low-sodium vegetable broth

3 cups trimmed and quartered Brussels sprouts

2 teaspoons Italian seasoning blend

1 teaspoon parsley

½ teaspoon ground black pepper

1 cup unsweetened coconut milk, or ½ cup coconut cream and ½ cup coconut milk for extra creaminess

1. In a large saucepan over medium heat, warm the oil. Cook the onion, bell pepper, and garlic, stirring frequently, for 5 minutes, or until soft.

2. Add the broth, Brussels sprouts, Italian seasoning, parsley, and black pepper and bring to a boil. Reduce the heat and simmer for 30 minutes, or until the sprouts are tender.

3. Add the coconut milk, then puree the soup using an immersion blender. (Or let the soup cool slightly, transfer to a blender, and, working in batches, puree until smooth. Reheat before serving.)

Per serving: 148 calories, 7 g fat (3 g saturated fat), 19 g carbohydrates, 6 g sugar, 214 mg sodium, 5 g fiber, 3 g protein

Did you know?

Coconut milk and coconut cream are made by boiling the coconut meat with coconut water. The difference between milk and cream is in the coconut concentration and the consistency: Coconut milk has the consistency of cow's milk and is made from simmering one part shredded coconut in one part water. Coconut cream is much thicker and richer. It is made by simmering four parts coconut in one part water.

BROCCOLI-CHEDDAR SOUP

MAKES 4 SERVINGS

This savory, creamy, comforting soup will become your go-to meal—mix up a batch in advance of Flo's arrival. Broccoli is loaded with vitamins A, B$_6$, C, and E and the minerals calcium, potassium, and magnesium. Spinach is high in calcium, which helps alleviate menstrual cramps. And Cheddar cheese contains calcium: Eating calcium-rich dairy products, especially those with added vitamin D, lowers the risk for developing PMS by as much as 40 percent.

2 tablespoons olive oil

1 onion, chopped

1 teaspoon sea salt, divided

1 teaspoon ground black pepper, divided

1 cup quinoa, rinsed

2 teaspoons minced garlic

7 cups low-sodium vegetable broth

5 cups chopped broccoli

1 large russet potato, peeled and chopped

3 cups spinach

2 tablespoons tahini

1 cup shredded Cheddar cheese*

1. In a large stockpot over medium heat, warm the oil. Add the onion, ½ teaspoon of the salt, and ½ teaspoon of the pepper and cook, stirring frequently, for 5 minutes, or until golden and tender.

2. Stir in the quinoa and garlic. Add the broth, broccoli, and potato. Bring to a boil and reduce the heat to a simmer. Cover and cook for 30 minutes.

3. Add the spinach, tahini, remaining ½ teaspoon salt, and remaining ½ teaspoon pepper. Cook, uncovered, for 4 to 5 minutes, or until the spinach has wilted.

4. Remove the soup from the heat, and let it cool slightly. Transfer it to a blender and puree in batches.

5. Return the pureed soup to the pot, add the cheese, and cook over low heat until the cheese has melted.

Per serving: 530 calories, 23 g fat (8 g saturated fat), 60 g carbohydrates, 6 g sugar, 859 mg sodium, 9 g fiber, 20 g protein

❋ Vegan? You can substitute vegan Cheddar-style shreds. Note that the protein content in vegan cheese is lower than in dairy cheese. In addition, most vegan cheeses contain little calcium and vitamin D, so you need to get them elsewhere in your diet. Fortified soy products and dark leafy green vegetables are excellent sources of calcium, and fortified soy milk is a good source of vitamin D.

SUPER 'SHROOM SOUP

MAKES 4 SERVINGS

Mushrooms are high in iron, a critical nutrient that helps increase fertility. Women who increase iron intake during the preconception period have a higher fertility rate than women who are iron deficient. Turmeric contains curcumin, which has proven estrogenic activity (meaning it imitates the activity of estrogen). Blend up this savory soup and share it with your significant other when you're ready to start trying to conceive!

2 tablespoons olive oil

3 large shallots, sliced

½ teaspoon salt + additional to taste

3 cloves garlic, chopped

2 teaspoons dried thyme

2 teaspoons dried sage

⅓ teaspoon ground turmeric

¾ pound shiitake mushrooms, stemmed and chopped

1½ pounds oyster mushrooms, chopped

5 cups water + additional for blending

3 teaspoons tamari + additional to taste

Ground black pepper

1. In a medium pot over medium heat, warm the oil. Add the shallots and cook, stirring frequently, for 5 minutes, or until light brown. Add the ½ teaspoon salt and the garlic and cook, stirring, for 3 to 4 minutes.

2. Stir in the thyme, sage, and turmeric. Then add the mushrooms.

3. Add the 5 cups of water and bring to a boil over high heat. Cover the pot and simmer for 20 minutes, or until the mushrooms are tender.

4. Remove the pot from the heat. Let the soup cool down, then transfer it in batches to a blender and blend until smooth. Add ½ cup of additional water at a time as needed to achieve a thick and creamy consistency.

5. Return the blended soup to the pot and stir in the 3 teaspoons of tamari and black pepper to taste. Taste and adjust the seasonings, adding additional tamari, salt, and pepper, if desired.

Per serving: 195 calories, 8 g fat (1 g saturated fat), 28 g carbohydrates, 6 g sugar, 514 mg sodium, 6 g fiber, 10 g protein

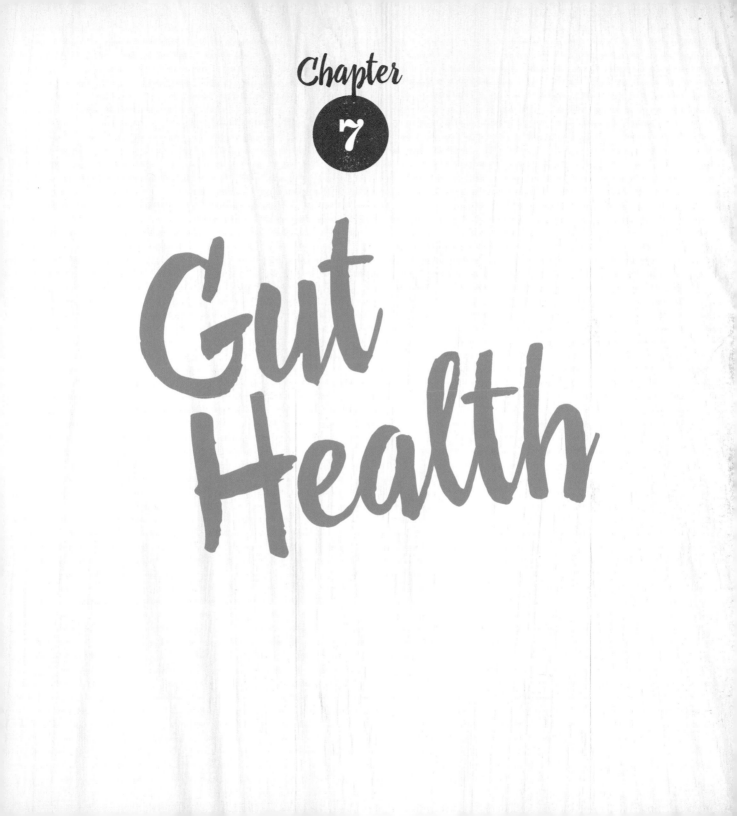

Chapter

7

Gut Health

Soothe a Troubled Tummy

There is nothing worse than feeling bloated, gassy, constipated, or all three—especially on a regular basis. Maybe you have a long Google search history on these topics or maybe you're too embarrassed to even ask your laptop, but the truth is, millions of women suffer from chronic digestive issues. And while some foods can certainly trigger a quick end to a great date, there are plenty of foods that won't upset your stomach and can actually help ease painful or humiliating symptoms. Don't let these funky feelings get in the way of your life! In this chapter, we'll show you how to incorporate the right combination of nutrients and important gut-friendly additives like fermented foods so you can balance your belly bacteria and feel great every day.

COMMON TUMMY TROUBLES

A study at New York University's Langone Medical Center in 2013 found that 74 percent of Americans were living with digestive symptoms like diarrhea, gas, bloating, and abdominal pain. Whether you've had the occasional bout of stomach cramps or suffer from chronic irritable bowel syndrome (IBS), there are steps you can take to manage your digestive system and make sure your gut is in good shape. We've compiled some of the most common issues, along with simple nutritional advice to help keep your stomach soothed and satisfied. Good gut health is increasingly linked to *overall* health, so it's important to make sure that your whole body is operating at its best.

Indigestion

Put simply, indigestion occurs when our stomach cannot process food properly. We've all binged on fast food or a superheavy meal and felt the regret bubble up that night in the form of indigestion—belching, bloating, diarrhea, nausea, vomiting, acidic taste in the mouth, heartburn, and a growling stomach. Ugh! The key is to listen to your body. If you've eaten something that doesn't

agree with you, try the Healing Peach Smoothie on page 175 for a quick detox to get you back up and running quickly. Caffeine and highly acidic foods can also exacerbate indigestion, so avoid these while you're on the mend.

There's a serious connection between our minds and our physical wellness, and sometimes indigestion is caused by other factors, such as anxiety, constipation, depression, pregnancy, stress, smoking, ulcers, alcohol use, medications (such as aspirin and pain relievers), and overeating during stressful times. That's why getting enough exercise and even incorporating meditation into your daily habits can be a huge help if you suffer from chronic indigestion or IBS. You can also try the Berry Probiotic Smoothie on page 172 to help soothe your stomach and keep you happy and humming both inside and out.

Gas

The truth is, *everybody farts*. There, we said it! It's not a glamorous topic, but flatulence is totally normal and occurs when excessive gas forms in the intestine and/or stomach while digesting

Parsley isn't just a garnish! It contains a high enzyme content that contributes to improved overall digestion and the effective elimination of waste. Parsley also helps relieve water retention, bloating, indigestion, and flatulence.

foods. A few reasons why we become gassy are swallowed air, eating too fast, lactose intolerance, and the inability of certain foods to be digested. You might even have specific trigger foods or be intolerant of certain foods, like dairy, soy, or gluten. Some foods make us *all* gassy. We recommend avoiding the following on a date night, before a presentation, or during a road trip with friends: asparagus, artichokes, beans, broccoli, corn, lactose, lentils, onions, pears, peas, and foods high in fiber.

GERD

GERD, also known as gastroesophageal reflux disease, occurs when the stomach's contents back up into the esophagus. It's similar to heartburn, and it can be pretty painful. GERD can be triggered by foods that have a high acidity level like coffee, citrus, tomato, and soft drinks. If you feel a burning in your stomach and esophageal tract after eating these foods, try to avoid them. In order for our bodies to process food in a comfortable and healthy way, we need good gut bacteria that come from eating foods like artichokes, bananas, broccoli, beans, and fermented foods like kimchi and kombucha. Try the Creamy Corn Chowder on page 181, which lacks acidity and has healing ingredients like tofu and probiotics.

IBD, IBS, *WTH*?

IBD (inflammatory bowel disease) is a broad term that refers to diseases that cause inflammation of the intestines. It's not so fun to think about, and even less fun to experience! Be careful not to confuse IBD with irritable bowel syndrome (IBS). IBD and IBS have similar symptoms, such as cramping and diarrhea, but the underlying disease process is different. IBD is the inflammation or

FOODS FOR A BALANCED BELLY

- **Kefir:** This smooth, slightly tangy, drinkable yogurt contains different types of live active cultures. It's 99% lactose free, making it easier to digest than cow's milk for those with lactose intolerance.
- **Fermented vegetables:** pickled carrots, green beans, and beets; lacto-fermented pickles; traditionally cured Greek olives
- **Fermented soybeans:** miso, natto, tempeh
- **Cultured dairy products:** buttermilk, yogurt, kefir, cheese
- **Cultured nondairy products:** yogurts and kefirs made from organic soy, coconut, etc.
- **Fermented grains and beans:** lacto-fermented lentils, chickpeas, miso, etc.
- **Fermented beverages:** kombucha, for example
- **Fermented condiments:** raw apple cider vinegar, etc.

destruction of the bowel wall, which can lead to super-painful ulcerations and narrowing of the intestines. IBS is a disorder of the gastrointestinal (GI) tract for which no obvious cause can be found—but you're not alone if you suffer from it. IBS affects between 25 million and 45 million people in the United States, and roughly two out of three sufferers are women. If you're nodding your head, please read on. We've got lots of delicious, satisfying recipes for you to sip that will soothe your stomach.

There are also different types of IBD, like Crohn's disease and ulcerative colitis. These disorders cause the destruction of the digestive system and can be truly life-altering illnesses. It's not uncommon for doctors to prescribe medication to help with inflammatory bowel disease, but it's still key to eat a powerfully healthy diet! What makes IBD really tricky is that it can decrease the body's ability to absorb nutrients, so it's especially important to eat lots of fresh fruits and vegetables. To help with symptoms, avoid certain foods like those high in acidity, and incorporate more probiotics into your diet, like those found in yogurt.

PASS THE PROBIOTICS!

You've probably heard about probiotics before, in yogurt advertisements or on those mysterious-looking kombucha bottles popping up on grocery store shelves next to coconut water and green juices. Probiotics are the "good bacteria" found naturally in some foods like yogurt, and also in our digestive system. Probiotics are your gut's best friend because they reduce inflammation and promote digestion-supporting bowel regularity, reduce harmful bacteria, and enhance our immune systems. Foods that contain probiotics are kefir, kimchi, pickles, sauerkraut, tofu, yogurt, dark chocolate, miso soup, and microalgae (ocean-based plants such as chlorella, spirulina, and blue-green algae) supplements. You can also buy probiotic supplements. Some of these names may sound funny, but these guys do a heck of a job making your system work properly!

Fun facts about …
KEFIR

Gut-Loving Nutrients

If you're a health nut, you may have already heard of kefir. Kefirs are a bacteria/yeast mixture that forms into "grains" and then is typically combined with cow's milk, goat's milk, or coconut milk to make a fermented drink. While that may not sound particularly delicious, we swear it is! Kefir has a tart, yogurtlike flavor that is creamy and smooth. What's even better than kefir's flavor is that it's full of amazing nutrients like probiotics and good bacteria to promote a healthy gut and digestion. We included it in some of the recipes in this chapter, but this creamy addition can be incorporated into any smoothie for amazing benefits!

KEFIR
(pronounced KEE-fer)

… originated in the Caucasus Mountains in eastern Europe. It's commonly believed that the name comes from the Turkish word *keif*, which means "good feeling"— we would agree!

HOW IT'S MADE

Kefir looks a little bit like small clumps of cauliflower about the size of wheat grains. Adding kefir to any milk (cow's, sheep's, almond or coconut milk, etc.) ferments the drink. That means that it chemically breaks down its host (the milk) into a substance of yeast and bacteria. The kefir grains are typically added to the milk for a period of time, and then removed with a strainer. What's left is a fermented product. Normally, you might associate bacteria or yeast with negative things, but actually our gut loves the bacteria in kefir and other fermented foods.

Bring It On Home

While kefir is still mostly popular across eastern and northern Europe, it is gaining steam in the United States and Japan, mainly because kefir is more powerful than yogurt as a probiotic. Kefir has significantly more good bacteria and yeast, making it the queen of gut health!

FIGHT OSTEOPOROSIS

Your gut is irrelevant without strong bones to hold you up! Osteoporosis is a big concern for women, and our bone tissue can start to deteriorate when we are as young as our twenties. For better bones, think calcium—specifically, kefir. It's a great source of calcium and vitamin K_2. Drinking kefir helps our bones increase their calcium absorption, which helps improve bone density and prevents possible fractures. If you have osteoporosis or are at risk of developing it, try the following smoothies and soups made with kefir, milk, and other nutrient-packed ingredients for extra strength and stamina.

BERRY PROBIOTIC SMOOTHIE

MAKES 1 SERVING

When you increase good bacteria in the gut, your digestion improves. You need to create a healthy microbiome inside your GI tract—and kefir is the perfect ingredient to help do just that. Spinach, blueberries, and flaxseeds are all good sources of dietary fiber, which promotes regular bowel movements—you see where we're going with this one.

1 cup frozen blueberries

1 cup spinach

1 cup plain unsweetened kefir

1 tablespoon natural nut butter

1 tablespoon ground flaxseeds

In a blender, combine the blueberries, spinach, kefir, nut butter, and flaxseeds. Blend until the desired consistency is reached.

Per serving: 389 calories, 20 g fat (6 g saturated fat), 39 g carbohydrates, 26 g sugar, 165 mg sodium, 8 g fiber, 16 g protein

Did you know?

Spinach also contains phytonutrients that prevent bacterial overgrowth in the gut microflora and decrease inflammation in the digestive tract. You barely taste it in this berry beauty!

PINEAPPLE YOGURT SMOOTHIE BOWL

MAKES 2 SERVINGS

Pineapple contains bromelain, a compound that helps process and break down proteins, which can often be difficult for the body to digest. The yogurt contains active cultures that increase good gut bacteria and improve digestion. Layer 'em together with banana and coconut for a tropical treat!

1 cup chopped fresh, frozen, or canned pineapple

6 ounces vanilla or coconut Greek yogurt or coconut milk yogurt

1 banana

½ cup pineapple juice or coconut water

TOPPINGS

1 tablespoon slivered almonds

1 tablespoon shredded coconut

1 tablespoon ground flaxseeds

In a blender, combine the pineapple, yogurt, banana, and pineapple juice or coconut water. Blend until the desired consistency is reached. Pour into a bowl and top with the slivered almonds, shredded coconut, and ground flaxseeds.

Per serving: 523 calories, 11 g fat (4 g saturated fat), 92 g carbohydrates, 63 g sugar, 56 mg sodium, 9 g fiber, 20 g protein

HEALING PEACH SMOOTHIE

MAKES 1 SERVING

Ginger contains chemicals called gingerols and shogaols that stimulate production of saliva, bile, and stomach fluids. Sounds gross, we know, but these chemicals decrease stomach contractions and can help improve muscle tone in your intestines. Blend up this anti-inflammatory wonder for a quick recovery when you're feeling queasy or have a stomachache.

2 cups frozen peaches

1 cup coconut water

½ cup low-fat plain or vanilla yogurt

½ cup plain unsweetened kefir

1 frozen banana

2" piece of fresh ginger, peeled

In a high-speed blender, combine the peaches, coconut water, yogurt, kefir, banana, and ginger. Blend until the desired consistency is reached. Enjoy immediately.

Per serving: 384 calories, 5 g fat (3 g saturated fat), 80 g carbohydrates, 57 g sugar, 384 mg sodium, 10 g fiber, 15 g protein

Did you know?

Peaches are a member of the rose family and are beneficial for digestion since they have a diuretic effect. Peaches also have a natural comforting effect and can ease a sour stomach. Peaches originated in China and are a symbol of good luck, protection, and longevity.

AVOCADO MINT SMOOTHIE

MAKES 1 SERVING

Mint not only smells great, it's a soothing herb that can help ease an upset stomach. Mint increases bile secretion and encourages bile flow, which speeds and eases digestion. When you combine it with the bromelain found in pineapple, you've got a refreshing smoothie that tastes great and settles an upset tummy quickly.

1 avocado

1 large frozen banana

1 cup probiotic coconut water

½ cup frozen pineapple chunks

¼ cup chopped parsley

6 mint leaves

1 teaspoon grated fresh ginger

In a blender, combine the avocado, coconut water, banana, pineapple, parsley, mint, and ginger. Blend on the highest speed until super smooth.

Per serving: 422 calories, 22 g fat (4 g saturated fat), 59 g carbohydrates, 29 g sugar, 268 mg sodium, 16 g fiber, 6 g protein

FLAT BELLY SMOOTHIE

MAKES 1 SERVING

The apple cider vinegar in this recipe is actually a *prebiotic*—not to be confused with *probiotics*. Prebiotics are a source of food for beneficial bacteria, helping maintain the population of good gut bacteria and keeping your digestive system healthy. Blending this prebiotic with the healing properties of ginger, cucumber, and coconut water makes for a smoothie that keeps bloat at bay.

1 cucumber, peeled and sliced

1 frozen banana

½ cup coconut water

Handful of ice

1" piece of fresh ginger, peeled and sliced

1 tablespoon apple cider vinegar

In a blender, combine the cucumber, banana, coconut water, ice, ginger, and vinegar. Blend until super smooth. Enjoy!

Per serving: 156 calories, 1 g fat (0 g saturated fat), 37 g carbohydrates, 20 g sugar, 133 mg sodium, 6 g fiber, 3 g protein

❋ DIY mouthwash: Mix ½ tablespoon of apple cider vinegar with 1 cup of water, then swish in your mouth. This antiseptic breaks down plaque and the bacteria that cause bad breath.

GI JANE
SWEET POTATO SOUP

MAKES 4 SERVINGS

This soup blends the active cultures in yogurt along with the dietary fiber found in onions and lentils for a creamy, filling meal that also helps maintain optimal digestive health.

1 tablespoon olive oil

1 onion, chopped

3 cloves garlic, chopped

1 large sweet potato, peeled and chopped

2 carrots, chopped

1 cup low-sodium vegetable broth

1 cup cooked lentils (can be canned, but drain and rinse)

1 cup spinach

1 avocado

½ cup plain 2% Greek yogurt

2 tablespoons chopped fresh dill

½ cup chopped cashews, for garnish

1. In a large saucepan over medium heat, warm the oil. Cook the onion and garlic for about 5 minutes, stirring frequently, until golden brown.

2. Add the sweet potato and carrots and cook, stirring, for 3 to 4 minutes.

3. Add the broth and bring to a simmer. Cook for 15 minutes, or until the vegetables are tender. Stir in the lentils.

4. Let the soup cool slightly, transfer it to a blender in batches, and blend with the spinach, avocado, yogurt, and dill until smooth.

5. Serve warm, topped with a sprinkling of the cashews.

Per serving: 295 calories, 16 g fat (3 g saturated fat), 30 g carbohydrates, 8 g sugar, 175 mg sodium, 10 g fiber, 11 g protein

Did you know?

The essential oils present in dill help stimulate and activate your digestive system and can help relieve constipation—so keep this recipe handy the next time you feel less than regular!

CREAMY CORN CHOWDER

MAKES 4 SERVINGS

This fiber-rich soup helps keep you regular, and the tofu and miso paste introduce healthy bacteria to your gut (trust us, this is a good thing!)—making this soup a perfect option for those who may need help coping with IBS or other intestinal illnesses.

1 tablespoon olive oil

½ onion, chopped

2 cups fresh or frozen corn kernels

1½ cups low-sodium vegetable broth

¼ cup silken tofu

1½ tablespoons white miso paste

1. In a large saucepan over medium heat, warm the oil. Add the onion and cook, stirring frequently, for 5 minutes, or until translucent. Add the corn and continue to cook, stirring, for 3 to 4 minutes.

2. Transfer the onion and corn to a blender. Add the broth, tofu, and miso paste. Blend until smooth. (For a thicker soup, add more tofu; for a thinner soup, add more broth.)

3. Pour the blended soup back into the pan and reheat before serving.

Per serving: 129 calories, 5 g fat (1 g saturated fat), 19 g carbohydrates, 6 g sugar, 305 mg sodium, 2 g fiber, 4 g protein

Did you know?

Miso paste is a probiotic food that contains millions of microorganisms similar or identical to the beneficial bacteria that live in your large intestine.

GIRLS GOT GUTS SOUP

MAKES 4 SERVINGS

Sweet potatoes and pumpkin are both good sources of dietary fiber, and the live cultures in kefir make this a deliciously robust, good-for-you soup.

¼ cup olive oil

1 onion, chopped

2 ribs celery, chopped

3 cloves garlic, minced

2 sweet potatoes, peeled and chopped

1 small baking pumpkin, peeled, seeded, and chopped

4 cups low-sodium vegetable broth

2 tablespoons honey

½ teaspoon ground allspice

½ teaspoon ground nutmeg

2 cups plain unsweetened kefir

1. In a large saucepan over medium heat, warm the oil. Cook the onion, celery, and garlic, stirring frequently, for 5 to 7 minutes, or until soft. Stir in the sweet potatoes and pumpkin and cook for about 7 minutes, until they begin to soften

2. Add the broth, honey, allspice, and nutmeg. The broth should almost cover the vegetables. If it doesn't, add a little water.

3. Cover and simmer for 30 to 40 minutes, or until the vegetables are tender. Remove from the heat. Let the soup cool slightly, then transfer to a blender and blend in batches.

4. Pour the soup back into the saucepan and stir in the kefir. Reheat and serve warm.

Per serving: 363 calories, 18 g fat (5 g saturated fat), 44 g carbohydrates, 25 g sugar, 257 mg sodium, 4 g fiber, 8 g protein

COOLING CUCUMBER-YOGURT SOUP

Cucumbers are not only refreshing in beauty products (or on your eyes), they are high in two elements needed for healthy digestion: water and fiber. This chilled soup is perfect to serve on hot, uncomfortable days, or anytime you're feeling less than comfortable.

2 large seedless cucumbers, chopped

1 avocado

½ cup plain 2% Greek yogurt

½ cup plain unsweetened kefir

½ cup red seedless grapes

3 scallions, coarsely chopped

¼ cup chopped red onion

Juice of 1 lemon

Salt and ground black pepper

In a blender, combine the cucumbers, avocado, yogurt, kefir, grapes, scallions, onion, lemon juice, and salt and pepper to taste. Blend until the desired consistency is reached. Chill in the refrigerator for at least an hour. Serve cold.

Per serving: 138 calories, 7 g fat (2 g saturated fat), 15 g carbohydrates, 9 g sugar, 153 mg sodium, 4 g fiber, 6 g protein

✳ If you struggle with acid reflux, drinking water can suppress its symptoms by raising your stomach's pH levels, and water-rich cucumbers can have the same effect. Try mixing up a pitcher of cucumber water to keep on hand in the fridge.

Kicking Cancer's Butt

Recipes That Lower Your Risk

Cancer can be tricky and vicious, and because researchers and scientists are still working to fully understand the many intricacies of the disease, it's especially important to eat healthy and take care of our bodies in every way. The term *cancer* is used to describe more than 175 diseases in which abnormal cells divide without control and invade other tissues. There are many different causes of cancer, including chemicals, radiation, genetics, viruses, and smoking. Sometimes, even after successful remissions, cells are able to hide and then resurface somewhere else in the body. Soups and smoothies are a great way to eat more healthy food so your body can keep on keeping on.

Lifestyle changes that can decrease your cancer risk include avoiding indoor tanning, limiting alcohol, protecting your skin from the sun, avoiding tobacco use, limiting red meat, eating a diet rich in fruits and vegetables, maintaining a healthy weight, and being physically active. We love soups and smoothies because they're loaded with fruits and vegetables that defend our bodies from free radicals and other cancer-causing toxins. Eliminating poor-quality foods and adding more soups and smoothies to your diet could be lifesaving. So what're you waiting for? Let's get our healthy on!

TOP CANCER FIGHTERS

Antioxidants

We've talked a lot about antioxidants throughout this book. That's because our bodies need them to prevent and repair cell damage. According to the National Cancer Institute, one-third of all cancer deaths may be diet related. This chapter will give you recipes containing cancer-fighting nutrients like antioxidants, which are critical in preventing cancer. An antioxidant is a molecule that prevents the oxidation of other molecules. Oxidation is a chemical reaction that produces free radicals, leading to cell damage. By consuming antioxidants such as ascorbic acid (vitamin C), you can stop these reactions, and in turn keep your cells healthy.

Vitamin C

What's the first thing that comes to mind when you think of vitamin C? Orange juice? Citrus fruit? Vitamin C, also known as ascorbic acid, is found in many vegetables and fruits. It's a powerful antioxidant that helps the body form and maintain connective tissue, including bones, blood vessels, and skin. It's also great for fighting colds and maintaining immunity.

But vitamin C is more than just a cold fighter. It is also an antioxidant that helps to prevent the formation of cancer-causing compounds. Diets high in vitamin C have been linked to a reduced risk of cancers of the stomach, colon, esophagus, bladder, breast, and cervix. Vitamin C fights free radicals and neutralizes the effects of nitrites, which are those nasty preservatives found in packaged or processed foods. As a general rule, you should stay away from overly processed foods if you want to maintain a baseline of good health and stay cancer free. If you're on the go and think grabbing a microwave meal is the answer, try a soup or smoothie from this book. It's just as quick and easy, we promise, and promotes a healthy body and brain. Swapping your packaged meals for one of our recipes will show you how good healthy looks and feels!

Folate

Another powerful cancer-fighting nutrient is folate. Folate, an essential B vitamin found in many foods, is needed by our bodies to make genetic materials. Folate is needed for repairing cells and making DNA—the genetic instructions for the body—and for forming red and white blood cells. We have added folate-rich foods to many of our recipes, like the Chocolate Berry-Nut Smoothie on page 198, to ensure you're getting a crazy-big dose of goodness—not to mention that this recipe is practically a dessert.

Vitamin E

Another free radical crusher is vitamin E, an antioxidant that protects against cell damage. You might be wondering how we come in contact with free radicals. The answer is that it happens all the time! We are exposed to free radicals from cigarette smoke, air pollutants, and ultraviolet light from the sun. So how do we protect ourselves? We need the good nutrients mentioned in this chapter and interspersed throughout the recipes in this book. Vitamin E is great for good health, and our body requires it to boost our immune system so it can fight bacteria and viruses.

By eating foods with vitamin E, you're also helping your body reduce its risk of cancer. Diets rich in vitamin E can prevent colon, liver, stomach, lung, and other cancers. Switch up your usual meal routine by eating recipes packed with vitamin E, like Swiss Chard Soup (page 209).

Beta-Carotene

Beta-carotene is another powerful anti-oxidant. Studies have shown that people who eat a diet high in beta-carotene—found primarily in orange and leafy green vegetables—have a reduced risk of cancer, particularly of the lung, colon, and stomach. Our Ready and Able Root Vegetable Soup (page 204) is loaded with beta-carotene and tastes fantastic on a chilly fall evening (or any time of the year, for that matter!).

FOODS THAT FIGHT CANCER

So now that you know what cancer fighters to eat more of, just where do you find them?

VITAMIN C is found in guava, bell peppers (all colors), oranges and orange juice, grapefruit and grapefruit juice, strawberries, pineapple, kohlrabi, papayas, lemons and lemon juice, broccoli, kale, Brussels sprouts, kidney beans, kiwifruit, cantaloupe, cauliflower, cabbage (all varieties), mangoes, white potatoes, mustard greens, tomatoes, sugar snap peas, snow peas, clementines, rutabagas, turnip greens, raspberries, blackberries, watermelon, tangerines, okra, lychees, summer squash, and persimmons.

FOLATE is found in fruits, legumes, and vegetables such as broccoli. Especially good sources are dark green leafy vegetables such as spinach, kale, and romaine lettuce. It is also found in chicory, oranges, papaya, nuts, beans, and peas.

VITAMIN E is found in almonds and almond butter, sunflower seeds and sunflower butter, wheat germ, hazelnuts, spinach, dandelion greens, Swiss chard, pine nuts, peanuts and peanut butter, turnip greens, beet greens, broccoli, canola oil, red bell peppers, collard greens, avocados, olive oil, and mangoes.

BETA-CAROTENE is found in sweet potatoes, carrots, kale, butternut squash, turnip greens, pumpkin, mustard greens, cantaloupe, red bell peppers, apricots, Chinese cabbage, spinach, lettuces (especially darker lettuces), collard greens, Swiss chard, watercress, pink and red grapefruit, watermelon, cherries, mangoes, tomatoes, guava, asparagus, and red cabbage.

THE BOTTOM LINE ON CANCER PREVENTION

You may be eating foods that actually *promote* cancer, while overlooking the powerful foods and nutrients that can *protect* you. A daily serving of processed meat increases your risk of colorectal cancer, while eating more fruits and vegetables can lower your risk. It's all about making small tweaks to your diet and lifestyle so that you *lower* your risk of disease. If you have been diagnosed, eating the right diet can help improve your outlook as well as support your medical treatment at this difficult time.

Why do we love soups and smoothies? Because a plant-based diet filled with a variety of vegetables, fruits, nuts, whole grains, and beans can help lower your risk for many types of cancer. Eating a colorful variety gives you the best protection. Plant-based foods are rich in nutrients that strengthen your immune system and protect against cancer cells. Fruits and vegetables are the best sources of antioxidants such as beta-carotene, vitamin C, vitamin E, folate, and selenium. These powerful nutrients protect against cancer and help the cells in your body perform optimally.

Listen: We want you to be your healthiest, happiest self, and while some cancers have a genetic component and may even be unavoidable, we want you to know that many cancers *can* be prevented. Our recipes are handpicked to fight so many health issues, from depression and anxiety to weight gain and cancer. It's pretty amazing that you can take control of your life by incorporating more healthy foods and nutrients into your diet.

Fun facts about ...
ACAI

Not Your Average Fruit

You're probably well versed on the world of berries. In the United States, we consume tons of strawberries, blueberries, raspberries, and blackberries every year. But how much do you know about acai (pronounced ah-sigh-EE)? It's a berry too—and one of the healthiest ones at that. Acai is commonly grown in subtropical regions like Central and South America, as well as in rain forests like those in the Amazon. That means it loves a warm, wet environment and is not typically grown in the United States. Acai berries grow on an acai palm tree that looks a little like those Miami or California palms you're used to seeing on TV or in magazines; however, on the acai palm, long purple chains of berries hang from the branches like beads. It's pretty amazing how nature changes from climate to climate. We're lucky that these delicious berries can be transported so that we can experience their luscious flavor and incredible health benefits. Check out our Berry Healthy Acai Bowl (page 203) for a tropical treat!

A Heart-Healthy Food

Acai helps lower cholesterol in our bloodstream due to its anthocyanins and antioxidants. When our blood vessels are relaxed, our heart can perform normally, without stress and strain. Adding a dose of acai to your weekly diet can help prevent heart disease, the leading killer in the United States. Try some acai berries in any of our smoothies for a punch of color and rich flavor!

THE TASTE OF GREAT HEALTH

Acai has been described as tasting like a cross between a blackberry and raspberry, mixed with a piece of dark chocolate. Yeah, our mouths are watering too. When ripe, these tasty little berries are a deep purple and can make your smoothie colorful and bright. But acai berries are way more than just a delicious snack. They're packed with incredible health benefits. We've laid them out here to give you more reasons to add them to your diet.

AN ANTIOXIDANT SUPERSTAR

While we're on the topic, acai has superpowers when it comes to fighting cancer. The berries are full of phytochemicals and anti-oxidants, which can slow and reverse the oxidative process associated with cancer and aging. These purple guys have about 10 times as many anti-oxidants as grapes, and 2 times the amount in blue-berries. Acai berries also improve cellular health because of their anthocyanins, which keep cells strong against free radicals. Basically, they are your best friend when it comes to fighting cancer-causing toxins.

AN IMMUNE BOOSTER

Acai berries also have an insane amount of vitamin C, which, as we mentioned before, is a pro at fighting cancer. According to a study in the *Journal of Agricultural and Food Chemistry*, the poly-phenolic compounds in acai reduced cancer cell proliferation by 56 to 58 percent. Acai berries also keep your immune system strong and can suppress colds and illness. If you feel a cold coming on, stock up on acai and get plenty of rest! It might just do the trick.

A HEALTHY SKIN PROMOTER

Have you ever seen a Brazilian glow? It might be because Brazilian people eat tons of acai berries since they grow easily in their climate. Acai and acai oil are great for glowing skin. Their antioxidants fight wrinkles and sun damage. What's better than that?

Will They Lead to Better Sex?

Acai has been linked to an increase in blood circulation, which, especially in men, can boost sex drive!

TROPICAL FRUIT SMOOTHIE

MAKES 1 SERVING

Mango and papaya both contain vitamin C, an antioxidant that helps prevent the formation of cancer-causing compounds. They also contain beta-carotene, a powerful antioxidant. Studies have shown that people who eat a diet high in beta-carotene have a reduced risk of cancer—so blend up this tropical treat as a way to power up your disease-fighting arsenal and stay healthy.

1 cup seeded and chopped fresh papaya

1 cup chopped frozen or fresh mango

½ cup unsweetened coconut milk

½ cup low-fat plain, vanilla, or coconut yogurt

In a blender, combine the papaya, mango, coconut milk, and yogurt. Blend until the desired consistency is reached.

Per serving: 239 calories, 3 g fat (1.5 g saturated fat), 49 g carbohydrates, 42 g sugar, 99 mg sodium, 5 g fiber, 8 g protein

Did you know?

Green, unripe papaya and papaya tree leaves contain an enzyme called papain. Papain has been used for thousands of years as a meat tenderizer and is an ingredient in current commercial meat tenderizers. In addition, injections of papain enzyme are given to treat herniated discs, and papain can be applied topically to treat burns, rashes, and cuts.

CHOCOLATE BERRY-NUT SMOOTHIE

MAKES 1 SERVING

Berries are loaded with vitamin C and other antioxidants that help prevent the formation of cancer-causing compounds, and red grapes are rich in antioxidant compounds called flavonoids that fight cancer cells. Combine those with the secret ingredient you won't even taste—spinach—for an extra boost of folate, an essential B vitamin needed for repairing cells, making DNA, metabolizing amino acids, and forming red and white blood cells. That's one powerful smoothie!

1 cup frozen mixed berries (blueberries, raspberries, strawberries)

1 cup coconut water or coconut milk

1 cup red seedless grapes

1 cup spinach

15 almonds

1 tablespoon unsweetened cacao powder

In a blender, combine the berries, coconut water or milk, grapes, spinach, almonds, and cacao powder. Blend for about 2 minutes and add water until the smoothie reaches your desired consistency.

Per serving: 328 calories, 10 g fat (1 g saturated fat), 63 g carbohydrates, 45 g sugar, 62 mg sodium, 10 g fiber, 8 g protein

Did you know?

Research shows that eating a vitamin E–rich diet reduces the risk of stomach, colon, lung, liver, and other cancers—and almonds are a great source of vitamin E. Toss a handful of almonds into any smoothie for extra cancer-fighting benefits.

C YOU NEVER, CANCER SMOOTHIE

MAKES 1 SERVING

This cancer-fighting green smoothie helps keep your body super strong with vitamin C–rich pineapple and orange, folate-rich spinach, and antioxidant superstar green tea, a great source of catechins, which fight cancer cell growth.

1 cup chopped pineapple

1 orange, peeled and chopped

1 cup spinach

1½ cups brewed green tea, cooled or chilled

In a blender, combine the pineapple, orange, spinach, and tea. Blend until the desired consistency is reached.

Per serving: 148 calories, 0 g fat (0 g saturated fat), 38 g carbohydrates, 29 g sugar, 16 mg sodium, 6 g fiber, 3 g protein

GOLDEN TEA SMOOTHIE

MAKES 1 SERVING

Antioxidants work by preventing the oxidative damage that leads to the formation of cancer cells—and green tea contains powerful antioxidants called catechins, which may prevent cancer. Additionally, this smoothie includes turmeric, the amazing spice that contains curcumin, which research suggests may help prevent or treat cancer by combating inflammation. But you won't need to worry about how that all works when you sip this refreshingly delicious cocktail!

1 cup berries of your choice (such as blueberries, raspberries, cranberries)

1 cup brewed green tea, cooled to room temperature

½ cup ice

1 teaspoon chia seeds

1 teaspoon honey, or to taste

½ teaspoon ground turmeric

In a blender, combine the berries, tea, ice, chia seeds, honey, and turmeric. Blend until the desired consistency is reached, adding more honey if desired.

Per serving: 127 calories, 2 g fat (0.5 g saturated fat), 29 g carbohydrates, 21 g sugar, 3 mg sodium, 5 g fiber, 2 g protein

Did you know?

The bottled brands of green tea have much lower antioxidant levels than home-brewed green tea. Researchers found as few as 3 milligrams of flavonoids in bottled teas, compared with up to 150 milligrams in the green tea made at home. Steep for 10 minutes to get the most health benefits.

PEACH CREAM SMOOTHIE

Raspberries and orange juice are both loaded with vitamin C and antioxidants, and peaches are high in beta-carotene. Studies have shown that people who eat a diet high in beta-carotene have a reduced risk of cancer. Who wouldn't want to eat more deliciously fresh, creamy fruit and yogurt—it's like a healthy ice pop in a glass!

1 large banana

1 peach, peeled, pitted, and chopped (or 1 cup frozen peaches)

1 cup fresh or frozen raspberries

1 cup fresh orange juice

6 ounces low-fat vanilla yogurt

In a blender, combine the banana, peach, raspberries, orange juice, and yogurt. Blend until smooth, adding more orange juice for a thinner smoothie.

Per serving: 484 calories, 4 g fat (2 g saturated fat), 105 g carbohydrates, 76 g sugar, 117 mg sodium, 14 g fiber, 14 g protein

Did you know?

Diets high in fruit may lower the risk of stomach and lung cancer.

BERRY HEALTHY ACAI BOWL

MAKES 2 SERVINGS

Acai berries contain compounds called flavonoids that have antioxidant effects. Added to the mix of other berries here, which are rich in vitamin C, they help to prevent the formation of cancer-causing compounds. Hi-ya! You can customize this yummy bowl however you'd like. We suggest lots of options to keep you healthy, alert, and going strong all day long.

2 packets (3.5 ounces each) frozen acai berry puree

1 frozen banana

¼ cup unsweetened coconut milk or almond milk

TOPPINGS

¼ cup raspberries, blackberries, or blueberries

¼ cup granola

2 tablespoons shredded unsweetened coconut

2 tablespoons slivered almonds

1 teaspoon chia seeds

In a blender, combine the acai berry puree, banana, and coconut milk. Blend until the desired consistency is reached. Pour into a bowl and top with any or all of the toppings!

Per serving: 592 calories, 35 g fat (12 g saturated fat), 62 g carbohydrates, 27 g sugar, 37 mg sodium, 14 g fiber, 13 g protein

READY AND ABLE
ROOT VEGETABLE SOUP

MAKES 4 SERVINGS

The carrots, sweet potatoes, and rutabaga in this savory soup are high in beta-carotene and vitamin C, both of which help fight cancer-forming compounds. Parsnips—which are available in most produce aisles—are high in folic acid and vitamin E, two additional cancer fighters. Serve up this rich root veggie soup whenever you're feeling the need for a boost of energy and strength.

2 carrots, chopped

1 parsnip, peeled and chopped

1 large sweet potato, peeled and chopped

1 rutabaga, peeled and chopped

4 cups low-sodium vegetable broth

1 cup canned light coconut milk

1 tablespoon pure maple syrup

1 teaspoon dried thyme

¼ teaspoon dried rosemary

1. Preheat the oven to 400°F. Cover 2 baking sheets with foil and spray each with olive oil cooking spray. Place the carrots and parsnip on 1 baking sheet and the sweet potato and rutabaga on the other.

2. Roast the vegetables for about 40 minutes, or until tender. (The carrots and parsnip may be done first, so keep an eye on them.) Remove from the oven and let cool.

3. Transfer the roasted vegetables to a blender and add the broth, coconut milk, maple syrup, thyme, and rosemary. Blend the soup until smooth and velvety. Heat before serving.

Per serving: 172 calories, 3 g fat (2.5 g saturated fat), 33 g carbohydrates, 15 g sugar, 213 mg sodium, 7 g fiber, 2 g protein

CREAMY WHITE BEAN-CAULIFLOWER SOUP

MAKES 4 SERVINGS

As you know by now, vitamin C is an essential antioxidant that helps to prevent the formation of cancer-causing compounds—and cauliflower helps deliver the goods in this filling recipe. Beans also contain antioxidants and phytochemicals, and research shows that bean consumption may reduce the risk of cancer too.

2 tablespoons olive oil

1 yellow onion, chopped

1½ teaspoons dried oregano

2 cloves garlic, minced

1 head cauliflower, cut into florets

½ teaspoon salt

½ teaspoon ground black pepper

5 cups low-sodium vegetable broth

1 pear, cored and chopped

½ cup canned cannellini beans, drained and rinsed

¼ cup rolled (old-fashioned) oats

1. In a large saucepan over medium heat, warm the oil. Cook the onion and oregano, stirring frequently, for 5 minutes, or until the onion is soft. Add the garlic and cook, stirring, for another minute.

2. Stir in the cauliflower. Season with the salt and pepper.

3. Add the broth, pear, beans, and oats. Bring to a boil, then lower the heat and simmer for 10 minutes, or until the cauliflower is tender.

4. Allow the soup to cool slightly, then use an immersion blender or upright blender to puree the soup until smooth. Heat before serving.

Per serving: 208 calories, 8 g fat (1 g saturated fat), 30 g carbohydrates, 10 g sugar, 597 mg sodium, 8 g fiber, 6 g protein

SHE'S A FIGHTER SOUP

MAKES 4 SERVINGS

This deliciously sweet-savory recipe combines carrots, which are high in beta-carotene, with the superspice turmeric to help keep you healthy and disease-proof. A dollop of Greek yogurt makes this an extra-special treat when you're craving something creamy and oh-so-satisfying.

2 tablespoons olive oil

1 cup chopped yellow onion

2 teaspoons ground turmeric

2 cloves garlic, minced

1 pound carrots, finely chopped

2½ cups low-sodium vegetable broth

1 tablespoon honey

1 tablespoon lemon juice

⅛ teaspoon ground allspice

Salt and ground black pepper

½ cup plain 2% Greek yogurt, for garnish

1. In a large saucepan over medium heat, warm the oil. Cook the onion, stirring frequently, for 5 minutes, or until soft. Add the turmeric and garlic and stir for 3 minutes.

2. Add the carrots and broth. Bring to a boil, then reduce the heat, cover, and simmer for 20 minutes, or until the carrots become very tender.

3. Remove the soup from the heat and let it cool slightly. Working in batches, puree in a blender until smooth.

4. Pour the blended soup back into the pan and whisk in the honey, lemon juice, and allspice. Season to taste with salt and pepper and heat before serving.

5. Pour into soup bowls and garnish with a dollop of yogurt.

Per serving: 177 calories, 8 g fat (1.5 g saturated fat), 23 g carbohydrates, 13 g sugar, 251 mg sodium, 4 g fiber, 4 g protein

SWISS CHARD SOUP

MAKES 4 SERVINGS

Swiss chard is popular for a reason: It contains folate, an essential B vitamin needed for repairing cells, making DNA, metabolizing amino acids, and forming red and white blood cells. Swiss chard also contains beta-carotene, an antioxidant, and vitamin E, both of which help reduce cancer risk. Blend up this powerful veggie into this uber-healthy green soup!

2 tablespoons olive oil

1 onion, chopped

2 cloves garlic, crushed

1 pound Swiss chard, center ribs and stems removed, leaves chopped

3½ cups low-sodium vegetable broth

1 cup chopped flat-leaf parsley

½ cup chopped fresh cilantro

¼ cup fresh mint leaves

1 teaspoon ground nutmeg

1 tablespoon lemon juice

Salt and ground black pepper

Plain 2% Greek yogurt, for serving

1. In a large saucepan over medium heat, warm the oil. Cook the onion and garlic, stirring frequently, until the onion is translucent. Stir in the chard, broth, parsley, cilantro, mint, and nutmeg.

2. Bring to a boil, reduce the heat, and simmer for about 15 minutes, or until the chard is tender.

3. Stir in the lemon juice and season to taste with salt and pepper.

4. Let the soup cool slightly. Working in batches, puree the soup in a blender until smooth.

5. Pour the blended soup back into the pan and heat before serving with a dollop of yogurt.

Per serving: 124 calories, 7 g fat (1 g saturated fat), 12 g carbohydrates, 4 g sugar, 450 mg sodium, 4 g fiber, 3 g protein

POWER-UP SOUP

MAKES 4 SERVINGS

Tomatoes and bell peppers are both loaded with vitamin C *and* beta-carotene, anti-oxidants that help prevent the formation of cancer-causing compounds. Let them help protect you with this super-easy-to-make soup.

2 large red bell peppers

1 tablespoon + ¼ cup olive oil

3 large heirloom tomatoes, stemmed, seeded, and cut into large chunks

5 leaves fresh basil

1. Preheat the oven to 400°F. Line a baking sheet with parchment paper.

2. Place the peppers on the prepared baking sheet and roast the peppers for about 1 hour, turning every 15 minutes, until charred on all sides.

3. Remove the peppers from the oven, put them in a bowl, and cover and allow to cool for 20 minutes. Peel the peppers, remove the stems and seeds, and cut them into chunks.

4. Meanwhile, heat 1 tablespoon of the oil in a large saucepan, then add the tomatoes and basil leaves. Cook, stirring frequently, for 15 minutes.

5. Let the tomatoes cool slightly, then puree them with the pepper in a blender. Add the remaining ¼ cup oil and continue to puree until the desired consistency is reached. Heat before serving.

Per serving: 199 calories, 17 g fat (2.5 g saturated fat), 10 g carbohydrates, 7 g sugar, 10 mg sodium, 3 g fiber, 2 g protein

Bone & Joint Health

Get Flexible,
Stay Strong

We may not think about our bones and joints because we can't see them, but our skeleton and connective tissue quite literally hold us together! As we age, daily life—not to mention gravity—takes a toll on our bones and joints. While many of us don't think about the structural health of our bodies until it's too late—we sprain an ankle, or worse, break something—it's critical to take care of our foundation so that we maintain a vibrant, healthy shape and good posture as we age. This chapter focuses on foods that increase your intake of calcium and antioxidants, as well as vitamin D and other nutrients that help keep your bones and joints healthy and strong.

STAND STRONG FOR LIFE

Bones reinforce your body and allow movement. They protect your brain, heart, and other organs from injury. Although we think of bones as hard and brittle, bone matter is actually living, growing tissue. Bones have cells that are continually renewed and grow stronger with a healthy diet. Bones are made primarily of calcium and collagen, which make them strong and flexible.

Until the age of 30, we build up calcium in our bones efficiently. After that, we stop adding new bone tissue—which eventually leaves many women over the age of 50 at risk for osteoporosis. The worst thing about weak bones isn't just bad posture, either. One in five people with a hip fracture dies within a year of the injury. One in three adults who fracture a hip stays in a nursing home for a year or more after the injury. The really scary part is that most people don't realize they have deteriorated bones until one breaks. At this point, it is difficult to strengthen your bones again.

The amount of calcium in your bones is the gauge of how strong they are. Your muscles and nerves require calcium and phosphorus, and if you don't consume enough, your body will take these minerals from your bones. In fact, calcium is deposited and withdrawn from your bones every day! However, eating the right foods will help you maintain the bone tissue you have and keep you standing strong and healthy for years to come.

TOP TIPS TO KEEP YOUR BONES STRONG

- Consume calcium, which is found in foods like milk, leafy green vegetables, and soybeans.

- Make sure you get enough vitamin D, either from foods, limited sun exposure, or supplements, because vitamin D helps your body absorb calcium.

- Stay active! Walking, especially uphill (whether hiking or climbing stairs), helps strengthen your bones.

FIGHT INFLAMMATION WITH FOOD

Inflammation is part of the body's immune response. White blood cells release chemicals into the blood to protect your body from harmful substances. This chemical release increases the bloodflow to the injured or infected area and causes warmth and redness. When fluid leaks into the tissues, swelling occurs. This affects your bones and joints because increased amounts of cells and inflammatory substances within the joint cause irritation, swelling of the joint lining, and wearing down of the cartilage that cushions the ends of your bones.

Joint swelling is typical with various types of arthritis, infections, and injuries. A swollen joint is a symptom of the following conditions.

OSTEOARTHRITIS is the "wear-and-tear" arthritis that happens with age or injury. There is a wearing down of the cartilage that cushions the ends of the bones. Swelling occurs in joints that support weight over a lifetime, such as knees, hips, feet, and the spine.

RHEUMATOID ARTHRITIS is an inflammatory arthritis that can happen at any age. It causes painful, stiff, and swollen joints.

We can't heal without inflammation, but when it is severe, it can actually damage the body. Chronic inflammation is the cause of many diseases, including cancer, obesity, and heart disease. Many foods contain nutrients that reduce inflammation, such as phytochemicals, which are natural chemicals found in plant foods. Spices in particular have been found to be effective at suppressing the inflammatory response. A few of these anti-inflammatory spices are cloves, ginger, rosemary, and turmeric, but the top 10 are highlighted on the following page. Shiitake mushrooms also contain compounds with the ability to suppress inflammation, such as ergothioneine, which prevents oxidative stress. Many inflammatory diseases begin in your gut, due to an imbalanced microbiome. Fermented foods such as kefir, kimchi, miso, tempeh, pickles, sauerkraut, olives, and other fermented vegetables will help replenish your gut's beneficial bacteria. Try our Cinnamon Cherry Smoothie (page 228) for a kick of cherry and turmeric, a double duty combo that fights inflammation.

TOP 10 MOST POTENT ANTI-INFLAMMATORY HERBS AND SPICES

A study published in the *Journal of Medicinal Foods* found a direct correlation between the antioxidant content of herb and spice extracts and their ability to prevent heart disease and premature aging. Cloves were ranked as the most potent of 24 common herbs and spices. The following were the top 10 most potent anti-inflammatory herbs and spices.

1. Cloves
2. Cinnamon
3. Jamaican allspice
4. Apple pie spice
5. Oregano
6. Pumpkin pie spice
7. Marjoram
8. Sage
9. Thyme
10. Gourmet Italian spice

JUST SAY NO TO OSTEOPOROSIS

Osteoporosis is a disease in which your bones lose minerals (like calcium) and become so porous and weak as a result that they become frail and more likely to break from a minor injury. The most common bones broken due to osteoporosis are the hips, spine, and wrist. The best way to keep bones strong is by consuming enough calcium and vitamin D.

The good news is that many foods contain the calcium, vitamin D, magnesium, and vitamin C that are critical for bone health.

Dairy Products

Dairy products, like milk, Greek yogurt, and hard cheeses, are excellent sources of vitamin D and calcium, which actually work together to maximize absorption in your body. If you don't eat dairy, you can definitely get your calcium intake through vegetables such as collard greens, turnip greens, kale, okra, Chinese cabbage, dandelion greens, mustard greens, and broccoli.

Minerals

Magnesium is a mineral that also plays an important role in maintaining healthy bones. It supports increased bone density and prevents the onset of osteoporosis.

Magnesium is found in spinach, beet greens, okra, tomato products, artichokes, plantains, potatoes, sweet potatoes, collard greens, and raisins. Potassium is another mineral that may also be beneficial for strengthening bones. It's found in raisins, potatoes, spinach, sweet potatoes, papaya, oranges, orange juice, bananas, plantains, and prunes.

RISK FACTORS FOR OSTEOPOROSIS

- **Family history:** Heredity is one of the top risk factors for osteoporosis. If your parents or grandparents had signs of osteoporosis (such as a fractured hip after a minor fall), you may be at greater risk.

- **Gender:** Women more than 50 years old have the highest risk of getting osteoporosis. Women are four times more likely than men to develop it due to their thinner bones and longer life spans.

- **Age:** Bone mass begins to decline after age 30.

- **Ethnicity:** Caucasian and Asian women are more likely to develop osteoporosis.

- **Bone structure and body weight:** Petite and thin women have an increased risk of developing osteoporosis because they have less bone to lose than women who weigh more and have larger frames.

- **Cigarette smoking:** Smoking puts you at higher risk of having osteoporosis and fractures.

- **Certain diseases:** Some diseases, such as rheumatoid arthritis, increase osteoporosis risk.

- **Certain medications:** Some medications, such as prednisone, increase your osteoporosis risk.

Vitamin C

Vitamin C is also beneficial for osteoporosis. Antioxidants ward off oxidative stress, therefore protecting against inflammation. Inflammation leads to bone destruction, which takes calcium away from the bones. Vitamin C helps slow that destruction. Foods high in vitamin C are red bell peppers, green bell peppers, oranges, grapefruits, broccoli, strawberries, Brussels sprouts, papaya, and pineapples.

OSTEOARTHRITIS

Osteoarthritis is the most common form of arthritis. It occurs when the protective cartilage on the ends of our bones wears down as we age. Osteoarthritis can damage any joint in your body; however, it typically affects joints in your hands, knees, hips, and spine. Antioxidants found in fruits and veggies like apples, onions, shallots, and strawberries reduce joint inflammation and pain. Omega-3 fatty acids also ease joint pain and reduce morning stiffness.

In addition, a compound in olive oil called oleocanthal helps prevent inflammation, and vitamin C is beneficial for osteoarthritis because it helps build collagen and connective tissue. Excellent sources of vitamin C are citrus fruits, red bell peppers, strawberries, broccoli, cabbage, and kale. It's never too early to start thinking about your bones and joints. In fact, adding these vitamin-rich foods to your diet now might mean you'll never have to think about it!

MAGIC BEANS

While beans contain calcium, magnesium, fiber, and other nutrients, they are also high in substances called phytates. Phytates interfere with your body's ability to absorb the calcium that is contained in beans. You can reduce the phytate level by soaking dried beans in water for several hours and then cooking them in fresh water.

SUPERSTAR FOODS TO MAINTAIN HEALTHY BONES AND JOINTS

- Apples, onions, shallots, and strawberries reduce joint inflammation and pain.

- Citrus fruits, red bell peppers, strawberries, broccoli, cabbage, and kale contain vitamin C to build connective tissue.

- Collard greens, turnip greens, kale, okra, Chinese cabbage, dandelion greens, mustard greens, broccoli, and yogurt contain calcium.

- Mushrooms contain compounds with the ability to suppress inflammation.

- Cinnamon, cloves, ginger, rosemary, and turmeric are anti-inflammatory spices.

COLLAGEN: NOT JUST GOOD FOR SKIN

When you think collagen, you might think of that stuff they put in face cream to reduce wrinkles. But the truth is, collagen and collagen-boosting foods are great for your bones and connective tissue. That's because bones are made up of mineralized substances and collagen fibers. As we age, we start to lose bone density, so it's important to eat the right foods to maintain healthy bones.

It's never too early to start thinking about your bones and joints. Be sure to eat plenty of collagen-rich foods like artichokes (see our Adios, Arthritis Soup on page 233) and dark leafy greens as well as our superstar foods for bones and joints listed above.

Fun facts about...
GINGER

The Root with a Punch

When you think of ginger, you might think of holiday gingerbread men or those spicy slices that come on the side of your sushi order. The truth is, ginger can be used in an abundance of recipes, from soups and smoothies to tea to chicken and beef dishes. We call it a "worldly favorite" because ginger is used all over the globe and has been since ancient times. The ancient Chinese, Indians, Arabs, and Greco-Romans were known to use ginger. It has an incredible spicy taste, but also medicinal qualities such as helping with nausea, pain, and inflammation. Ginger's anti-inflammatory properties help eliminate arthritis symptoms and boost bone health. In this chapter, we added an amazing Ginger Citrus Smoothie (page 230) for you and your body to enjoy.

DIY GINGER TEA

Add 4 to 6 thin slices of peeled fresh ginger, lemon juice, and honey to a boiling mug of water for a delicious tea that helps with inflammation and nausea. It's also lovely on a snow day as a healthy alternative to hot chocolate!

Health Benefits

So why do we love ginger so much? It's because we love foods that taste great while also helping our bodies maintain good health. Ginger is super low calorie but is packed with nutrients to keep us healthy. You should consider eating ginger if you have an upset stomach, if you're experiencing inflammation or arthritis, or have morning sickness.

ANTI-INFLAMMATORY PUNCH

While we're on the subject, ginger is great for fighting inflammation. It contains compounds called gingerols, which help relieve pain for people with arthritis, therefore improving mobility. A study published by *Life Sciences* found that ginger is loaded with compounds that fight free radicals, which can cause painful inflammation of joints and bones. If you're experiencing joint pain, try spicing up your regular diet with fresh ginger.

STRONGER BONES

Ginger is a natural bone strengthener, according to a study conducted at the University of Miami. Researchers found that taking a regular ginger supplement promoted bone density and reduced inflammation. You don't have to take a supplement to see the effects; just start sipping one of our ginger-packed smoothies or soups on a regular basis.

OTHER SUPER BENEFITS

If you experience frequent nausea, ginger is your new best friend! A study done in the *British Medical Journal* found that ginger is more effective than dimenhydrinate (Dramamine) in reducing motion sickness. That's because ginger aids in digestion and soothes painful stomachaches.

Research presented at the Frontiers in Cancer Prevention Research, a huge meeting where cancer experts met in Phoenix in 2003, suggested that gingerols—the main ingredient in ginger—may inhibit the growth of colorectal cancer cells. Don't have cancer? Why not go ahead and prevent it? There are already so many other benefits to eating ginger, and it tastes amazing!

Savor the Side

You'll commonly find fresh ginger alongside sushi. It's the finely sliced pink condiment that accompanies wasabi, the spicy green one. More than just a pretty garnish, it adds a burst of flavor that makes its health wonders truly delicious!

AVOCADO-CHIA SMOOTHIE BOWL

MAKES 2 SERVINGS

The fresh kiwi and berries in this delicious bowl are high in vitamin C, which is beneficial for osteoarthritis because it helps build collagen and connective tissue. Throw in the mineral-rich spinach and the avocado, which contains antioxidants such as vitamin C and vitamin E, and you have a delicious combo that helps fight inflammation and lets you start your day off right!

1 avocado

1 cup spinach

1 cup unsweetened almond milk

1 teaspoon agave nectar or honey

TOPPINGS

1 kiwifruit, sliced

½ cup berries

2 tablespoons chia seeds

1 tablespoon chopped nuts

In a blender, combine the avocado, spinach, almond milk, and agave nectar or honey. Blend until the desired consistency is reached. Pour the smoothie into a bowl and top with the kiwi, berries, chia seeds, and nuts.

Per serving: 611 calories, 43 g fat (5 g saturated fat), 56 g carbohydrates, 21 g sugar, 215 mg sodium, 27 g fiber, 12 g protein

Did you know?

Nuts—such as almonds, walnuts, and cashews—contain omega-3 fatty acids that ease joint pain and reduce morning stiffness.

GRAPEFRUIT BONE BUILDER

MAKES 1 SERVING

Grapefruit not only has a refreshing, wake-me-up scent, it also contains vitamin C, which helps protect against oxidative stress and inflammation. Blend up this sweet-tart combo for a strong start to your day.

1 pink grapefruit, peeled and segmented

1 frozen banana

1 cup unsweetened almond milk

½ cup frozen strawberries

In a blender, combine the grapefruit, banana, almond milk, and strawberries. Blend until the desired consistency is reached. Enjoy!

Per serving: 277 calories, 4 g fat (0 g saturated fat), 63 g carbohydrates, 41 g sugar, 183 mg sodium, 9 g fiber, 5 g protein

CINNAMON CHERRY SMOOTHIE

MAKES 1 SERVING

Cherries get their color from plant chemicals called anthocyanins. Several studies have shown that cherries and cherry juice reduce inflammation. Plus the spinach in this smoothie is high in calcium, potassium, and magnesium, which all help keep your bones and joints strong and supple.

1 cup frozen cherries

1 cup coconut water

1 cup spinach

1 banana

1 tablespoon chia seeds

½ teaspoon ground turmeric

¼ teaspoon ground cinnamon

In a blender, combine the cherries, coconut water, spinach, banana, chia seeds, turmeric, and cinnamon. Blend until the desired consistency is reached and enjoy!

Per serving: 301 calories, 4 g fat (1 g saturated fat), 64 g carbohydrates, 39 g sugar, 270 mg sodium, 13 g fiber, 6 g protein

Did you know?

Chia seeds form a thick gel when soaked in water for about 30 minutes. This gel forms in the stomach when you eat chia seeds and slows the breakdown of carbohydrates into sugar! This means your blood sugars do not spike and you stay fuller longer.

THE INFLAMMATION TAMER

This yummy tropical combination ensures you'll start the day feeling like you're on the beach! The vitamin C in the mango and anti-inflammatory properties of turmeric and cinnamon combine to protect your bones and joints from weakness and pain.

1 cup unsweetened coconut milk

½ teaspoon ground turmeric

½ cup frozen mango chunks

⅓ teaspoon ground cinnamon

1 tablespoon unsweetened shredded coconut

In a blender, combine the coconut milk, turmeric, mango, cinnamon, and coconut. Blend until smooth and creamy. Enjoy!

Per serving: 150 calories, 8 g fat (8 g saturated fat), 20 g carbohydrates, 14 g sugar, 17 mg sodium, 4 g fiber, 2 g protein

DIY Coconut Milk

MAKES 4 CUPS

You can make homemade coconut milk from shredded coconut! Here's how.

4 cups water

2 cups unsweetened shredded coconut

1. In a medium pot over medium-high heat or in the microwave oven, heat the water until hot but not boiling.

2. Put the coconut in a blender and add the hot water.

3. Blend on high for 3 to 5 minutes, until thick and creamy.

4. Place a piece of cheesecloth or a fine-mesh strainer over a large bowl. Pour the coconut mixture through the cloth or strainer, straining out the solid pieces. The liquid in the bowl is coconut milk. (If using cheesecloth, squeeze out the extra milk before throwing out the solid pieces of coconut.)

5. Drink immediately or store in the fridge for up to 3 days. Shake before using, as the "cream" or "fat" of the coconut milk will rise to the top.

GINGER CITRUS SMOOTHIE

MAKES 1 SERVING

This zesty smoothie combines vitamin C–rich citrus fruit with the special spices turmeric and ginger, found to be effective at suppressing the inflammatory response. Blend up and drink with the confidence that you're helping your body stay strong and pain free all day.

1 cup fresh, frozen, or canned diced pineapple

1 cup coconut water

Juice of 2 oranges

½ large cucumber,* peeled and chopped

½ teaspoon ground turmeric

2" piece fresh ginger, peeled

In a blender, combine the pineapple, coconut water, orange juice, cucumber, turmeric, and ginger. Blend until the desired consistency is reached and enjoy!

Per serving: 228 calories, 1 g fat (0.5 g saturated fat), 55 g carbohydrates, 43 g sugar, 51 mg sodium, 4 g fiber, 4 g protein

✳ Cucumbers can be used to freshen your breath! Place a cucumber slice on the roof of your mouth to kill odor-causing bacteria.

SWEET POTATO AND PEAR SOUP

MAKES 4 SERVINGS

Sweet potatoes and carrots are high in antioxidants that reduce inflammation and pain. Simmer and blend this recipe with creamy Greek yogurt for a sweet-savory soup that suppresses bone loss and keeps you satisfied.

1 tablespoon olive oil

2 large carrots, chopped

¾ cup chopped celery

½ cup chopped onion

1 teaspoon ground turmeric

1 clove garlic, minced

5 cups low-sodium vegetable broth

2 sweet potatoes, peeled and chopped

2 pears, peeled, cored, and chopped

½ teaspoon salt

2 tablespoons honey

1 tablespoon lemon juice

1 cup plain 2% Greek yogurt

1. In a large stockpot over medium heat, warm the oil. Cook the carrots, celery, and onion, stirring frequently, for 5 minutes, or until the onions are translucent.

2. Add the turmeric and garlic and cook for a minute or two longer, stirring. Stir in the broth, sweet potatoes, pears, and salt. Then add the honey. Simmer for 40 minutes, or until the vegetables are soft. Remove from the heat.

3. Allow the soup to cool slightly. Working in batches, puree in a blender (or use an immersion blender). Add more broth for a thinner soup.

4. Pour the blended soup back into the pot, add the lemon juice, and stir. Reheat the soup, then whisk in the yogurt until combined. Serve warm.

Per serving: 261 calories, 5 g fat (1.5 g saturated fat), 48 g carbohydrates, 26 g sugar, 563 mg sodium, 7 g fiber, 7 g protein

Did you know?

Garlic doesn't just keep the vampires away. It has anti-inflammatory properties that protect against osteoarthritis too.

ADIOS, ARTHRITIS SOUP

MAKES 4 SERVINGS

Vitamin C–rich artichokes help produce collagen, which is essential for the health of our bones and connective tissues. They are also high in magnesium, which enhances the uptake and absorption of calcium. Blend them with potatoes, which are loaded with potassium, and you've got a hearty soup that's mega healthy too.

2 tablespoons olive oil

2 medium leeks, chopped

7 cloves garlic, chopped

2 cups low-sodium vegetable broth

2 cups water

1 package (10 ounces) frozen artichoke hearts, thawed

2 medium potatoes, peeled and chopped

4 sprigs fresh thyme

2 teaspoons lemon juice

Salt and ground black pepper

1. In a large stockpot over medium heat, warm the oil. Add the leeks and garlic and cook, stirring frequently, for 5 minutes, or until the leeks are softened.

2. Add the broth, water, artichokes, potatoes, and thyme. Cover and bring to a boil. Simmer, partially covered, for 25 minutes, or until the potatoes are tender.

3. Let the soup cool slightly, then remove the thyme sprigs. Transfer the soup to a blender and blend until smooth, working in batches if necessary.

4. Return the soup to the pot and stir in the lemon juice. Reheat. Add salt and pepper to taste before serving.

Per serving: 214 calories, 8 g fat (1 g saturated fat), 33 g carbohydrates, 5 g sugar, 149 mg sodium, 7 g fiber, 5 g protein

✱ Lemon juice can freshen your fridge and cutting boards. Take a cotton ball or sponge, dampen it with lemon juice, and leave it in the fridge for several hours to absorb odors. Get rid of your cutting board's odors and sanitize it at the same time by rubbing the cut side of half a lemon all over the board.

JOINT POWER SOUP

MAKES 4 SERVINGS

The superpower in this soup comes from broccoli and kale—excellent sources of calcium and vitamin C, both critical for bone and joint health. Prepare this in advance and add a cup to your meals during the week for an extra boost of bone strength and overall health!

1 tablespoon olive oil

1 leek, sliced

3 cloves garlic, crushed

½ head broccoli, chopped

4 leaves kale, chopped

1 zucchini, chopped

2 cups fresh or frozen peas

3 cups low-sodium vegetable broth

1 teaspoon dried parsley

1 teaspoon dried oregano

Salt and ground black pepper

1. In a large stockpot over medium heat, warm the oil. Cook the leek and garlic, stirring frequently, for 5 minutes, or until they are translucent.

2. Add the broccoli, kale, and zucchini and continue to cook, stirring, for 5 minutes. Add the peas and broth and bring to a boil.

3. Add the parsley, oregano, and salt and pepper to taste. Simmer for 10 minutes, or until the vegetables are soft.

4. Let the soup cool slightly, then blend using an immersion blender or stand blender. Reheat and serve warm.

Per serving: 154 calories, 4 g fat (1 g saturated fat), 23 g carbohydrates, 8 g sugar, 212 mg sodium, 7 g fiber, 7 g protein

✱ Consuming a cup of soup before meals can help with weight loss. It increases your satiety level and reduces hunger levels after meals. (You won't be as ravenous and likely to binge on empty calories, either.) A cup of soup as a starter is also a great way to sneak in some extra veggies!

CREAMY VEGGIE SOUP

MAKES 4 SERVINGS

This rich, savory soup combines a wealth of healthy veggies that help to protect your bones and joints. Mushrooms contain compounds that suppress inflammation, such as ergothioneine, which prevents oxidative stress.

SOUP

1 tablespoon olive oil

1 onion, chopped

1 pound (2 cups) chopped button mushrooms

1 large tomato, chopped

2 pounds butternut squash, peeled and chopped

1 tablespoon dried oregano

1 tablespoon low-sodium seasoning, such as Mrs. Dash

1 teaspoon ground turmeric

6 cups low-sodium vegetable broth

2 pounds Brussels sprouts, trimmed and sliced

1 pound spinach

Fresh lemon juice (optional)

CASHEW CREAM SAUCE

1 cup cashews

1 cup unsweetened almond milk

1. *To make the soup:* In a large stockpot over medium heat, warm the oil. Cook the onion, stirring frequently, for 2 to 3 minutes. Add the mushrooms and continue to stir. Add the tomato.

2. Add the squash, oregano, low-sodium seasoning, and turmeric to the pot. Stir in the broth. Bring to a boil, then simmer for 5 minutes.

3. Add the Brussels sprouts, spinach, and water as needed to cover. Simmer for 10 minutes, or until the squash and sprouts are cooked through.

4. Let the soup cool slightly, then blend it in batches until smooth. Pour the blended soup back into the pot and reheat it.

5. *To make the sauce:* Meanwhile, combine the cashews and almond milk in a blender. Blend until smooth. Stir the sauce into the soup, and serve hot. If desired, squeeze a little lemon juice on top before serving.

Per serving: 484 calories, 18 g fat (3 g saturated fat), 69 g carbohydrates, 17 g sugar, 422 mg sodium, 19 g fiber, 23 g protein

✳ For easier prep, look for presliced vegetables like mushrooms and Brussels sprouts. Or chop your veggies and prepare the soup over the weekend and refrigerate it for a healthy meal or snack at the ready all week long.

SWEET POTATO
BONE BROTH SOUP

MAKES 4 SERVINGS

Bone broth can help reduce joint pain and inflammation thanks to its chondroitin sulfates, glucosamine, and other compounds from the boiled-down bones. It can also act as an anti-inflammatory, thanks to its amino acids, and it contains high amounts of calcium and magnesium, which contribute to healthy bone formation. No wonder bone broth is so popular as a health remedy!

1 tablespoon olive oil

1 onion, chopped

3 medium cloves garlic, chopped

2 tablespoons peeled, sliced fresh ginger

1 teaspoon ground turmeric

3 cups bone broth*

2 cups sliced carrots

1 cup cubed sweet potato

²/₃ cup unsweetened coconut milk

Salt and ground white pepper

1. In a large saucepan over medium heat, warm the oil. Cook the onion, stirring frequently, for 5 minutes, or until soft. Add the garlic and ginger and continue to cook, stirring, for another minute.

2. Stir in the turmeric. Add the broth, carrots, and sweet potato and simmer for about 20 minutes, until the vegetables are tender.

3. Add the coconut milk and remove the pan from the heat. Let the soup cool slightly, then blend it in batches until smooth. Add salt and pepper to taste.

4. Reheat the blended soup before serving.

Per serving: 161 calories, 6 g fat (2.5 g saturated fat), 22 g carbohydrates, 9 g sugar, 216 mg sodium, 4 g fiber, 5 g protein

✳ You can find ready-made bone broth at most health food stores or you can make your own.

BAD-TO-THE-BONE SOUP

MAKES 4 SERVINGS

Mushrooms are amazing vegetables—not only do they taste earthy and rich, they contain compounds with the ability to suppress inflammation, such as ergothioneine, which prevents oxidative stress. Blended here with the unmistakably delicious aroma of rosemary, they create a healthy, savory soup that keeps you feeling great!

8 ounces baby bella mushrooms, quartered

8 ounces (2 large) portobello mushrooms, sliced

6 ounces shiitake mushrooms, stemmed and sliced

2 tablespoons olive oil

2 tablespoons apple cider vinegar

4 sprigs fresh rosemary

Salt and ground black pepper

5 cups cauliflower florets

3 cups mushroom broth, divided

1. Preheat the oven to 425°F. In a large bowl, toss the mushrooms with the oil, vinegar, rosemary, and salt and pepper to taste.

2. Spread the mushrooms out on a baking sheet. Roast for 15 minutes, or until they begin to caramelize around the edges. After roasting, they should still be moist.

3. While roasting the mushrooms, in a large pot over medium-high heat, boil the cauliflower in water to cover for 10 minutes, or until tender. Drain the cauliflower.

4. Add the cauliflower and about 2 cups of the mushroom broth to a blender. Blend on low until the cauliflower is smooth. Add some of the roasted mushrooms to the blender, reserving ¼ cup for a garnish. Continue adding broth and mushrooms until you like the consistency and flavor.

5. Serve warm and garnish with the remaining roasted mushrooms.

Per serving: 141 calories, 8 g fat (1 g saturated fat), 16 g carbohydrates, 6 g sugar, 523 mg sodium, 5 g fiber, 6 g protein

Chapter 10

Super Immunity

No More Sick Days!

Let's talk about immunity. What is it and why does it matter, anyway? Your immune system is that helpful bodily resource that resists infections and toxins and fights off illness. Do you remember as a kid when the winter flu was circling around school? Some kids never seemed to catch it, while others would be out for a week or two, unable to get out of bed. It happens to adults too! Every year a nasty cold seems to get passed around the office. So how do you avoid the plague? The key to fighting off or resisting these illnesses is to build up your immune system. It's your ultimate health booster. In this chapter, we've compiled some delicious recipes to keep you healthy all year round. You can say goodbye to pesky runny noses, painful body aches, chills, fevers, and all the other cold and flu symptoms.

EAT YOUR IMMUNITY

Our body is capable of fighting off invaders like pathogenic bacteria and viruses, and also of destroying cells when they become cancerous. This is all done through our powerful immune system. The main components of your immune system are the immune cells, the structural barriers in your body in which the majority of these cells are localized, and the specific messenger molecules that call the cells to action or tell them to stop. These immune system cells circulate in your bloodstream and in the lymph nodes.

But there are things that can weaken the system, especially poor nutrition. Poor nutrition leads to increased infections, slow healing, and increased susceptibility to illness complications. That means that what we put into our bodies is so incredibly important. It can make or break our ability to fight off nasty infections and illnesses.

It's probably no surprise that vitamin C is a germ-fighting rock star. It decreases the duration and severity of symptoms associated with upper respiratory infections and contributes to healthy T cell function. But don't ignore these other immunity-boosting foods:

GARLIC contains allicin, a natural chemical that fights bacteria and viruses.

CITRUS FRUITS are a great, tangy way to get vitamin C. It's a crucial antioxidant that supports your immune system. In addition to oranges, grapefruits, and other citrus fruits, you can get vitamin C from kiwifruit and strawberries.

HERBS AND SPICES have been shown to kill germs. Try curry, a mix of spices like chile peppers, turmeric, garlic, and ginger that curbs inflammation. Rosemary, oregano, and thyme are other herbs that provide antioxidants.

PROBIOTICS are the good bacteria that keep your gut healthy, which is great for your immunity. Choose kefir and yogurt. Look for "live cultures" on the label.

CAULIFLOWER, BROCCOLI, AND BRUSSELS SPROUTS are all cruciferous vegetables. In addition to antioxidant vitamins, they also contain choline. Choline keeps your cells functioning properly and also helps keep bacteria in the gut. Cauliflower contains glutathione, an antioxidant that fights off infection.

GREENS such as kale, spinach, and

Swiss chard are immune-boosting foods that contain high levels of vitamin C and help fight infection. They also contain folate, another immune booster.

MUSHROOMS are an excellent source of the immune-boosting mineral, zinc. Those who don't have enough zinc in their diet have fewer white blood cells to fight off disease, leading to a weakened immune response.

CINNAMON is antiviral, antifungal, and antibacterial. It fights the pathogens that cause illness.

CARROTS are an excellent source of beta-carotene, which supports the body's mucous membrane. This lines the respiratory and intestinal tracts, making it harder for bacteria to enter the bloodstream.

GINGER has chemicals called sesquiterpenes that target rhinoviruses, the most common category of cold viruses, as well as substances that help suppress coughing. Ginger is also a natural pain and fever reducer and a mild sedative.

ONION AND GARLIC, when combined, contain numerous antiseptic and immunity-boosting compounds, plus garlic helps to open clogged sinuses.

BLACK PEPPER, made from black peppercorns, is high in piperine, a compound known for its fever-fighting and pain-relieving qualities.

THE FLU VS. A COLD

It's sometimes hard to tell, but there's a difference between the flu and an ordinary cold. Both are respiratory infections caused by viruses, and their symptoms are often similar. So how can you determine what you have? Flu symptoms are typically more severe than cold symptoms and come on more quickly. A cold usually involves a combination of sneezing, coughing, and headache. If you are experiencing more than a couple of symptoms, it's more likely that you have the flu. Those suffering from a common cold are less likely to have a fever, and symptoms such as a runny nose or sore throat often improve within a few days.

Taking your temperature is the first step in determining if your illness is a cold or flu. Here are the other common flu symptoms:

OTHER COMMON FLU SYMPTOMS

- Feeling feverish or having a 100°F or higher fever; however, not everyone with the flu has a fever
- Headaches or body aches
- Vomiting, nausea, and/or diarrhea (particularly among children)

- Sore throat
- Cough
- Fatigue
- Chills
- A congested or runny nose

SOOTHING REMEDIES FOR COLDS AND THE FLU

So, those good memories of your mom giving you chicken soup when you were home sick aren't the only reasons that bowl was comforting. Research shows that sipping warm liquids such as tea, chicken soup, or warm apple juice speeds up the passage of mucus through the nose. This alleviates congestion and decreases the amount of time viruses are in contact with the lining of your nose. Plus, soup and other liquids help prevent dehydration—a major issue when you're under the weather. *Pro tip:* A cool-mist vaporizer or humidifier can add moisture to the air, which might loosen congestion. If nothing else, be sure to rest, drink fluids, and keep the air around you moist. Remember to wash your hands frequently as well!

THE BOTTOM LINE ON BOOSTING IMMUNITY

Look, nobody enjoys being sick. There's nothing worse than a stomach bug or the flu to keep you bed ridden and nauseous. That's why it's important to help your body protect itself. Your immune system is the root of your overall health.

When you are sick, your life is on hold. Rather than treating an illness after you have it, the best thing you can do is strengthen your immunity so you do not get sick in the first place! There are easy, preventive habits you can start doing now so you don't get sick later. For example, try incorporating probiotics into your diet to create a healthy digestive process.

You already know that the other key player in keeping you well is vitamin C. Consume vitamin C and nutrients that boost immunity by making some of the smoothies and soups in this chapter. Staying healthy goes beyond just a healthy diet. Be sure to get plenty of sleep, stay hydrated, and wash your hands! Take the advice from your school days. Hand washing is the number one preventive measure you can take to stay healthy and prevent illness!

Fun facts about …
GARLIC

Nature's Miracle Plant

Since ancient times, garlic has been used for a host of different things, from treating acne to repelling bugs to suppressing coughs. In fact, some say it's one of the healthiest, most versatile foods around! The ancient Egyptians, Babylonians, Greeks, Romans, and Chinese used garlic as medicine. Aside from its medicinal and curing properties, garlic adds a strong, delicious flavor to many savory dishes, especially soup! Garlic is also great for curing colds and boosting immunity. If you're under the weather, try some garlicky broth to ease sinus tension and help with pesky congestion. Our Cold Zapper Soup (page 259) should do the trick if you're unwell (or even if you're not!).

BONUS USE

Garlic is usually thought of as a food, but did you know that it can be used for minor glass repair? It's true! Garlic is a natural adhesive that, when crushed and filled into hairline cracks, can make glass smooth again.

HEALTH BENEFITS

Not sure what to turn to when you're sick, have a cold sore, a breakout, athlete's foot, or need to banish those annoying summer mosquitos? Garlic's got your back. It's that small, white, bulbous plant from the onion family, but it stands out as arguably the healthiest of the allium plants. We've put together a list of its superstar benefits for longevity and better overall health.

KICK YOUR COLD

Garlic is a well-known immunity booster. In a 12-week study done by the US National Library of Medicine, a daily garlic supplement reduced people's chance of getting a cold by 63 percent when compared to people taking a placebo. Cold symptoms were also found to last only 1.5 days rather than 5 days for the placebo takers. Adding garlic to your diet could significantly reduce your risk of catching that cold that circulates around your office every year. Who doesn't want to avoid that congestion? Those sniffles? That cough? We could go on.

FIGHT MEMORY LOSS

Garlic is also packed with antioxidants that reverse and prevent the free radical damage that speeds up the aging process. Nowadays, more and more people are experiencing that damage by getting diseases like Alzheimer's and dementia. The good news is that garlic supplementation has been shown to reduce the oxidative stress that causes memory loss. Garlic also helps regulate cholesterol and blood pressure, which may also help prevent these dreaded brain diseases. All in all, it has your brain's back and can help protect important memory function.

LIVE LONGER

We know now that garlic fights chronic illnesses like Alzheimer's and dementia, but it also fights immune system diseases, heart disease, and high cholesterol. These illnesses constitute the top reasons for mortality in the United States, and garlic is a master at defending your body from all of them! If living longer is something you'd like to do (we know we would!), you should consider adding garlic to your regular diet. It can be as easy as keeping a high-quality garlic powder in your cabinet and sprinkling it in soups or over poultry or even greens.

Did you know?

There are more than 300 varieties of garlic across the world. Try switching up your usual garlic buy for a fun twist of flavor!

GINGER BEET IMMUNE BOOSTER

We love combining flavors to make food an experience rather than just something to fill us up. The spiciness of ginger paired with the sweet, earthy flavor of beets makes for a superstar combination. But this smoothie is more than just delicious: It has some incredible nutrients to fight off illness and keep you healthy. Beets boost immunity through their vitamin C, folate, manganese, iron, and phytochemicals. Ginger has chemicals called sesquiterpenes that target rhinoviruses, the most common category of cold viruses, as well as substances that help suppress coughing. It's also a natural pain and fever reducer and a mild sedative. But don't let that sedative quality scare you. It just means it can knock out those awful cold and flu symptoms while it's in your system. If you feel a cold coming on, be sure to have this smoothie!

1 cup coconut water

1 cup spinach

1 apple, cored and seeded

1 lemon, peeled

1 small beet, scrubbed and quartered

½ cup ice

¼ cup fresh parsley

1 tablespoon chia seeds

½" piece of fresh ginger, peeled

In a blender, combine the coconut water, spinach, apple, lemon, beet, ice, parsley, chia seeds, and ginger. Blend until the desired consistency is reached.

Per serving: 252 calories, 4 g fat (0.5 g saturated fat), 56 g carbohydrates, 36 g sugar, 138 mg sodium, 13 g fiber, 6 g protein

❋ **Spinach**, an immune-boosting food, contains high levels of vitamin C and helps fight infection. It also contains folate, another immune booster.

Parsley is high in vitamin C and folate.

Lemon is high in vitamin C, a crucial antioxidant that supports your immune system.

BERRY COCONUT BLISS

MAKES 1 SERVING

When you're under the weather, or you feel like an illness is creeping in, be sure to eat lots of fresh berries. Berries are bursting with flavor and nutrients, from vitamin C to antioxidants that keep your insides running smoothly, and allow your body to focus on fighting off invaders like viruses. This smoothie is your best friend when it comes to immunity, and it tastes like dessert, but we promise it's healthy!

2 tablespoons dried goji berries

1 cup unsweetened coconut milk

½ cup blueberries

½ cup raspberries

½ cup blackberries

2 tablespoons unsweetened shredded coconut

2 Medjool dates, pitted

1 tablespoon ground flaxseed

1. Soak the goji berries in warm water for 15 minutes, then drain and discard the water.

2. In a blender, combine the coconut milk, berries, coconut, dates, and flaxseed. Blend until the desired consistency is reached.

Per serving: 455 calories, 16 g fat (11 g saturated fat), 77 g carbohydrates, 55 g sugar, 71 mg sodium, 17 g fiber, 8 g protein

 Did you know?

You can buy goji berries at most natural markets like Whole Foods. And remember, they're not just for sweet dishes, either! Adding goji to a savory dish gives any meal a surprise twist.

TROPICAL GREEN SMOOTHIE BOWL

This tropical-inspired treat is packed with immune-boosting spinach, which has high levels of vitamin C and folate. It also has kiwi, mango, and pineapple, which contain crucial antioxidants that keep your immune system strong. And finally, the probiotics in the kefir or yogurt have good bacteria to keep your gut healthy—another way to fight off illness.

1 cup baby spinach

½ cup frozen mango chunks

½ cup frozen pineapple chunks

½ cup plain unsweetened kefir or Greek yogurt

1 banana

TOPPINGS

2 tablespoons shredded coconut

1 kiwifruit, sliced

½ banana, sliced

1 tablespoon chia seeds

1. In a blender, combine the spinach, mango, pineapple, kefir or yogurt, and banana. Blend until thick and creamy. Pour into a bowl and let chill in the freezer for a few minutes.

2. Top the smoothie bowl with coconut, kiwis, bananas, and chia seeds.

Per serving: 482 calories, 12 g fat (7 g saturated fat), 93 g carbohydrates, 51 g sugar, 110 mg sodium, 16 g fiber, 12 g protein

Did you know?

Kiwis can be applied to your skin to get rid of excess oil, tighten pores, fade dark spots, and reduce wrinkles. Kiwis also contain alpha hydroxy acids and vitamins C, E, and K and are great for exfoliating the skin. Make a simple kiwi face mask by peeling two kiwis, chopping the fruit into small pieces, and mashing it. Apply the mashed kiwi to your face and neck, and wash it off after 15 minutes.

VITAMIN C COLD CRUSHER

MAKES 1 SERVING

This smoothie is packed with vitamin C and other amazing nutrients to fuel your body and arm your immune system when needed most. The orange juice and mango are stacked with vitamin C and other crucial antioxidants to support your immune system. Also included is kale, the superfood found everywhere these days, another immune-boosting food containing high levels of (you guessed it!) vitamin C to help fight infection. Kale also contains folate, another immune booster. The parsley and mint kick up the flavor and contain even more vitamin C to give you a boost when you're feeling down!

1¼ cups frozen mango chunks

1 cup orange juice

1 cup chopped kale, tough stems and ribs removed

2 medium ribs celery, chopped

¼ cup chopped flat-leaf parsley

¼ cup chopped fresh mint

In a blender, combine the mango, orange juice, kale, celery, parsley, and mint. Blend until smooth.

Per serving: 317 calories, 1 g fat (0.5 g saturated fat), 76 g carbohydrates, 57 g sugar, 102 mg sodium, 9 g fiber, 8 g protein

PEACHES 'N' CREAM

MAKES 1 SERVING

Peaches, strawberries, pineapple, and orange juice are the heroes in this blended treat. All are high in vitamin C to support a healthy body. We added yogurt packed with probiotics and good bacteria to keep your gut healthy, which is hugely beneficial for your immunity. Tip: Look for "live cultures" on the label!

1 cup frozen sliced peaches

1 cup frozen strawberries

1 cup fresh orange juice

6 ounces peach-flavored 2% Greek yogurt

½ cup frozen pineapple chunks

In a blender, combine the peaches, strawberries, orange juice, yogurt, and pineapple. Blend until smooth.

Per serving: 414 calories, 4 g fat (2 g saturated fat), 86 g carbohydrates, 69 g sugar, 52 mg sodium, 7 g fiber, 15 g protein

COLD ZAPPER SOUP

MAKES 4 SERVINGS

This easy-to-make, easier-to-eat soup mixes fragrant and delicious onion and garlic that, when combined, have numerous antiseptic and immunity-boosting compounds. Garlic also helps to open clogged sinuses. It's one of the top foods to help you when you're sick. We also included green chiles and sweet potatoes, both good sources of vitamin C and iron, crucial in red and white blood cell production for proper immune functioning. The mushrooms add a nice meaty bite and are an excellent source of the immune-boosting mineral zinc. Those who don't have enough zinc in their diet have fewer white blood cells to fight off disease, leading to a weakened immune response. Last but not least, goji berries contain compounds called polysaccharides, which strengthen the body's ability to fight disease. Gojis are also a good source of vitamin C and zinc, both of which protect against disease. You'll be coming back for more!

2 tablespoons olive oil

1 red onion, finely chopped

1 green chile pepper, finely chopped (wear plastic gloves when handling)

4 cloves garlic, minced

2 medium sweet potatoes, unpeeled and finely chopped

1 pint shiitake mushrooms, sliced

¼ cup dried goji berries

4–5 cups low-sodium vegetable broth

Salt and ground black pepper

1. In a large pan over medium heat, warm the oil. Cook the onion, chile, and garlic, stirring frequently, for 5 minutes, or until the onion softens.

2. Add the sweet potatoes, mushrooms, and goji berries to the pan. Stir and add enough broth to cover all the ingredients. Simmer for 15 minutes, or until the potato is soft.

3. Allow the soup to cool slightly, then transfer in batches to a blender and puree until smooth. Season to taste with salt and black pepper. Reheat and serve warm.

Per serving: 191 calories, 7 g fat (1 g saturated fat), 27 g carbohydrates, 11 g sugar, 277 mg sodium, 5 g fiber, 4 g protein

HEALING CARROT, DATE, AND GINGER SOUP

This warm soup is a delight when you're not feeling well. We recommend sipping it under your favorite blanket with a good book in hand. The garlic here fights bacteria and viruses, while the orange and carrots—both high in vitamin C—give you an important dose of immunity. As well, carrots have beta-carotene, which makes it harder for bacteria to enter your bloodstream (pretty powerful!). The ginger targets viruses too, and is a natural pain and fever reducer. With this healthy dose of onion and garlic, your immune system will be singing your praises—you might be able to sing again too, since it opens clogged sinuses.

2 tablespoons olive oil

2 cloves garlic, chopped

½ cup chopped onion

1 rib celery, chopped

1 teaspoon sea salt

1½ pounds carrots, chopped

3 cups low-sodium vegetable broth

3 cups water

4 dates, pitted

1 tablespoon grated orange peel

1 orange, peeled and chopped

1½" piece of fresh ginger, peeled

1. In a large stockpot over medium heat, warm the oil. Add the garlic, onion, celery, and salt and cook, stirring frequently, for 5 minutes, or until soft.

2. Add the carrots and cook, stirring, for a few minutes, then add the broth and water. Continue simmering for 10 minutes, or until the carrots are tender.

3. Let the soup cool slightly. Working in batches, transfer the soup to a blender and add the dates. Puree until smooth.

4. Add the orange peel, chopped orange and ginger and blend again. Heat before serving.

Per serving: 196 calories, 7 g fat (1 g saturated fat), 31 g carbohydrates, 17 g sugar, 631 mg sodium, 7 g fiber, 3 g protein

BOUNCE BACK ZUCCHINI-CAULIFLOWER SOUP

MAKES 4 SERVINGS

This nutrient-dense soup combines the goods of the garden with great cruciferous veggies. Cauliflower has choline, an essential nutrient that keeps your cells functioning properly and increases healthy bacteria in the gut. It also has glutathione, an antioxidant that fights off infection. The potatoes and lemon are a perfect juxtaposition of earthy and tangy, while the turmeric, onion, and garlic add a zing of intense flavor to wake up your sinuses.

1 tablespoon olive oil

1 small onion, chopped

3 cloves garlic, minced

¼ teaspoon ground turmeric

2 potatoes, peeled and chopped

½ head cauliflower, chopped

1 medium zucchini, chopped

2 large carrots, chopped

2 ribs celery, chopped

Salt and ground black pepper

Juice of 1 lemon

4 cups low-sodium vegetable broth

¼ teaspoon ground red pepper

1. In a large pot over medium heat, heat the oil. Add the onion, garlic, and turmeric, and cook, stirring frequently, for 5 minutes, or until the onion becomes translucent.

2. Add the potatoes, cauliflower, zucchini, carrots, celery, salt, and black pepper to taste. Cook, stirring, for a few minutes. Stir in the lemon juice.

3. Add the broth and red pepper and bring to a boil. Cover and simmer for 15 minutes, or until the veggies are soft.

4. Allow the soup to cool before blending. Use an immersion blender, or add the soup to a blender in batches. Puree until smooth.

5. Return the soup to the pot and heat before serving.

Per serving: 183 calories, 4 g fat (1 g saturated fat), 33 g carbohydrates, 8 g sugar, 621 mg sodium, 6 g fiber, 5 g protein

SINUS-CLEARING SPINACH CURRY SOUP

MAKES 4 SERVINGS

Between the curry and black pepper, this soup isn't lacking in flavor or spices. But it's more than just an awakener for your taste buds—all the ingredients here are perfect for supporting immune health. Spinach fights infection and boosts immunity through its vitamin C and folate. Curry powder helps curb inflammation, and black pepper has piperine, a compound known for its fever-fighting and pain-relieving qualities.

1 tablespoon olive oil

1 small onion, chopped

4 cups spinach

1 cup low-sodium vegetable broth

½ cup cooked great Northern beans

½ teaspoon curry powder

⅛ teaspoon ground black pepper

1. In a medium saucepan, warm the oil. Cook the onion, stirring frequently, for 5 minutes, or until soft.

2. Add the spinach, cover the pan, and cook for 3 to 4 minutes, or until the spinach is wilted.

3. In a blender, combine the cooked spinach and onion with the broth, beans, curry powder, and pepper. Blend until smooth and serve warm.

Per serving: 73 calories, 4 g fat (1 g saturated fat), 8 g carbohydrates, 1 g sugar, 51 mg sodium, 2 g fiber, 3 g protein

Beans are good for you, but they can make you gassy. It is important to realize that gas production is a normal bodily process. Some of the benefits of gas-producing fiber fermentation in the gut include improved mineral absorption, especially of calcium and magnesium, and enhanced immunity. You can reduce the gas by soaking dry beans before cooking and replacing the water several times.

GARLIC-LEEK COLD REDUCER

MAKES 4 SERVINGS

As you've probably noticed, we're packing these immune-boosting soups with garlic. It's fantastic for health and is also one of the world's most flavorful additions to any savory meal. And garlic is a natural bacteria and virus fighter. The carrots and black pepper in this recipe are great for respiratory health as well. With this soup, you will be back on track to good health.

1 head garlic

3 tablespoons olive oil + additional for drizzling on the garlic

1 large leek, thinly sliced

Salt

3 carrots, sliced

4 ribs celery, sliced

½ teaspoon chopped fresh sage

2½ cups low-sodium vegetable broth, divided

2 cups unsweetened cashew milk

1 cup canned navy beans, rinsed and drained

½ teaspoon ground black pepper

1. Preheat the oven to 400°F. Cut the top off the head of garlic, so the top of each clove is exposed, and drizzle a little oil on top. Wrap the whole garlic head in foil, place on a baking sheet, and bake for 1 hour, or until golden.

2. Heat the 3 tablespoons of oil in a large stockpot over medium heat. Add the leek and a pinch of salt. Cook, stirring frequently, for 5 minutes, or until soft. Add the carrots, celery, and sage and cook for 15 minutes, or until the vegetables are tender.

3. Pour in 2 cups of the broth, along with the cashew milk, beans, and pepper. Simmer uncovered for 15 minutes, until the beans are soft and the soup is thick.

4. Add 1 cup of the bean soup to a blender with the remaining ½ cup broth and 6 cloves roasted garlic. Blend until smooth.

5. Stir the blended soup back into the pot with the unblended soup. Add salt to taste. Serve warm.

Per serving: 236 calories, 12 g fat (1.5 g saturated fat), 26 g carbohydrates, 5 g sugar, 230 mg sodium, 8 g fiber, 5 g protein

11 Healthy Habits to Start Now

As a registered dietitian, people ask me all the time what to do to be healthy. Since I started practicing 20 years ago, I've seen all kinds of diet trends and patterns—some good, some bad—but most healthy habits remain the same. So when I teamed up with *Women's Health* to write this book, we decided to join forces and give you our very best eat-right advice. On the following pages, you'll find our top tips—all backed by real research—for optimizing health. Even better, they're completely realistic, so you'll actually be able to stick with them and feel great every day.

1. EAT OFTEN

Nearly all experts stress the importance of eating frequently to keep your metabolism and energy up and to avoid becoming so ravenous that you overeat when you finally do sit down to a meal. The "three meals plus two snacks a day" approach appears to be the best one for weight loss and weight maintenance. In a study in the *Journal of the Academy of Nutrition and Dietetics*, researchers found that people who were at a healthy weight and those who had lost weight both regularly ate two snacks a day. Snacking also appears to prevent weight gain. In one study, researchers followed more than 2,300 girls for 10 years (from about age 10 to age 20). Those who ate less frequently had an average increase of 1 body mass index unit and $\frac{1}{2}$ inch in waist size more than girls who ate six times a day.

How does eating often help? There's really no evidence to support the belief that it keeps your metabolism humming, but the opposite is absolutely true. If you cut back too far on calories, you're embarking on a self-defeating proposition: The lack of calories slows your metabolism. Plus, if you're only eating three times a day and trying to be calorie conscious, there is a good chance that you won't eat enough.

Probably the biggest benefit of eating often comes from the effect it has on blood sugar (glucose) levels and, therefore, insulin production. When glucose and insulin are in balance, your appetite is on an even keel. That not only helps reduce hunger but also simply makes you feel better. I know from personal experience that having small meals throughout the day (instead of three squares) keeps me energized. Some experts think that eating at regular intervals leads to less fat storage, too, because your body learns to recognize that food will be available relatively soon. And psychologically, knowing that your next meal isn't far away helps you cope with the biggest fear of people trying to lose weight: the fear of being hungry.

Of course, what you put in your mouth matters. If your snacks consist of potato chips and cupcakes, you aren't doing your health or your waistline any favors. As you'll see, many of our snacks are more like mini-meals. That's because we see snacking as the perfect opportunity to sneak more nutrients into your diet—and little portions of "real" foods are far more satisfying than the empty calories you'd get from chips and candy. In a study from the University of Illinois, women who had two snacks a day had a higher intake of fiber than those who noshed less often. Additionally, women who snacked in the afternoon had a higher intake of fruits and vegetables than those who snacked in the morning. But don't worry, we've got your fruit and veggie intake covered with our delicious recipes.

2. PAIR CARBS WITH PROTEIN OR FAT

Carbs are not evil. They're essential fuel, and they're your body's preferred energy source. On top of that, foods that are classified as mostly carbs—whole grains, fruits, vegetables—come packed with vitamins, minerals, and phytochemicals that are important for disease prevention. They can also be high in fiber, which helps keep you feeling full and satisfied. However, when you eat carbs by themselves, your body converts them into glucose faster than it would if you were eating something that slowed digestion (such as protein or fat) at the same time. An elevated glucose level causes a spike in insulin, which leads to a crash in blood sugar, which then results in extreme hunger. If that happens on a regular basis, your body switches to starvation mode, slowing your metabolism to conserve energy.

Translation: You burn fewer calories in everything you do.

When you do choose carbs, make them complex carbs whenever possible. That means whole grains instead of white refined ones for bread, pasta, and rice. That's because refined carbs, like white flour and sugar, are chemically closer to glucose, and therefore they break down quickly. The fiber in whole grains and fruit slows this process somewhat, but the effect could be blunted even more if you combined your carbs with some protein or fat. (Beans and vegetables are a little different. Beans are mostly carbs, but they pack a hefty dose of protein, too. And except for potatoes, corn, and peas, the carbs in vegetables are comparatively minimal, even in those that are "sweet," like beets, carrots, and winter squash.)

3. DON'T FEAR FAT.

According to a survey from the International Food Information Council, just 20 percent of people think that all fats are equal when it comes to health, but 67 percent try to cut as far back on all fats as they can. That's a mistake, because how much fat you eat doesn't really have an impact on your weight or your risk for disease. It's the type of fat and the total calories you take in that really matter.

There are four general categories of fat: polyunsaturated, monounsaturated, saturated, and trans. With the exception of trans fat, your body needs all of them. Fat is a major component of every cell in your body. It helps you absorb fat-soluble nutrients from low-fat foods, keeps your skin and hair healthy, and makes your brain work more efficiently. Some types of polyunsaturated and monounsaturated fats also protect against disease and control inflammation. Saturated fat raises cholesterol levels and also increases your odds of developing insulin resistance (which can lead to diabetes), but you still need some of it in your diet. Cholesterol, which is primarily made from saturated fat, is an important building block for hormones.

Trans fat should be avoided, period. Studies show that as little as 1 gram of trans fat a day increases your odds of developing heart disease. Steering clear of it is far easier when you follow a diet that contains few packaged foods. The biggest source of trans fat is partially hydrogenated vegetable oil, which is found in crackers, cookies, cakes, and other processed foods. Many manufacturers have cut it from their products, as evidenced by the labels screaming "Trans Fat Free!" Still, always read the ingredients list, looking for the words "partially hydrogenated." Food manufacturers are allowed by law to say that something is trans fat free if it contains less than 1 gram of trans fat. When all it takes is 1 gram a day to put your health at risk, though, you can't afford to "accidentally" eat three half-gram portions.

One big problem with low-fat diets is that people tend to replace the missing fat with carbs. A body of research done at Harvard University as well as other institutions has shown that this swap unfavorably changes cholesterol levels: "Bad" LDL rises and "good" HDL drops. Replace saturated fat with polys or monos, and you get the opposite outcome. Eating a diet relatively high in unsaturated fats also lowers blood pressure more than a diet relatively high in carbs does.

A study funded by the National Institutes of Health found that low-carb and low-GI (glycemic index) diets helped people who lost weight to keep it off. The participants ate three different diets for 4 weeks each. The low-carb diet supplied just 10 percent of calories from carbohydrates. The low-GI diet was similar to a traditional Mediterranean diet—40 percent of the calories came from fat, 20 percent from protein. In the low-fat diet about 20 percent of the calories came from fat. The results: The participants burned an average of 300 and 150 more calories a day on the low-carb and low-GI diets, respectively, than they did on the low-fat diet. This was probably because the low-carb and low-GI diets did a better job of keeping blood sugar levels stable and insulin spikes minimal.

You might be wondering why, if the low-carb diet revved calorie burn twofold, we don't suggest you eat that way. Two reasons: Low-carb diets can be notoriously difficult to stick with for life—not for everyone, but for a lot of people. In addition, such a high-protein diet often means a lot of meat. Meat comes with saturated fat, so the impact on your heart health is problematic.

Here's another important point to keep in mind: Fat makes food taste good. On the one hand, that can cause you to overeat, but on the other, it can help you eat more vegetables and other healthy foods that you should be getting in your diet. I'm pretty sure that even the most strident vegetable lover would admit that a little olive oil, Parmesan cheese, toasted nuts, or even—wait for it—butter on top of steamed asparagus likely makes the asparagus more flavorful.

4. NEVER SKIP BREAKFAST

Skip the morning meal and chances are good that you'll end up consuming more calories overall simply because you are hungrier. Think about it: If you finish dinner at 7:00 p.m. and don't eat again until noon the next day, you have gone without food for 17 hours. You think you're helping yourself drop pounds because you're cutting out calories, but you're actually causing your body to store more fat because it doesn't know when the next influx of energy is coming. In addition, eating breakfast has been associated with lower blood glucose and cholesterol levels, and skipping it is linked to constipation and menstrual pain. In children, breakfast helps boost attention span and learning. (It's not clear if adults get the same benefit.) Studies have consistently shown that breakfast eaters weigh less than breakfast skippers. Some studies have found that people who have a high-protein meal, like eggs, are more satisfied, while others show that whole grain cereal is most filling. Some of the research suggests that you should have a lot of calories at breakfast, while some says a light meal is what's called for. None of these studies is conclusive, so our advice is to just eat something, preferably a carb-fat or carb-protein combo.

5. NEVER EAT STANDING UP

At one point or another, we have all stood in front of the refrigerator with the door open, eating leftovers or ice cream right out of the container. And even if you aren't guilty of this little healthy eating blooper, I'll bet you've eaten a meal while doing something else—like watching TV or answering e-mail—that diverts your attention from what you're putting in your mouth. It's a habit that many of our experts have broken, because when you don't concentrate on your food as you're eating it, it doesn't quite register in your body. You could call it calorie amnesia: You can't really remember what you ate, so you don't get as much satisfaction from it. As a result, you find yourself craving something else not long after your meal. The science bears this out. In a study in the *American Journal of Clinical Nutrition*, researchers had one group of participants eat a meal while playing computer solitaire and another group eat without any distractions. The solitaire group had a hard time remembering what they ate, and they felt less full. What's more, they ate twice as much when cookies were offered half an hour later.

No matter how busy you are, you can afford to take 15 minutes to sit down and eat your meal. Focus on the food on your plate, and really notice the aromas, flavors, and textures. Eating your meal slowly helps too. Japanese researchers found that fast eaters have triple the risk of being obese as those who take their time.

6. SPEND TIME IN THE KITCHEN

Learning to cook changed my health for the better. I can control the nutritional quality and calorie counts of my meals. I also found that cooking with my son makes him more likely to try different foods—an observation backed up by a study from the University of Alberta, which found that children who helped with food prep were about 10 percent more inclined to like vegetables.

To say that restaurant portions tend to be large is an understatement. On average, the typical restaurant meal has 50 percent more calories than a home-cooked meal. But those calories aren't the only worrisome things you're being served: A survey of restaurant meals by the RAND Corporation uncovered the sad fact that 96 percent of the nearly 30,000 chain restaurant menu items tested exceeded daily saturated fat and sodium recommendations. And don't think the local bistro is any healthier: Chefs use a lot of salt, oil, and butter in their cooking, and big portions are just as common in independent restaurants.

Cooking at home does not mean that you have to be the next Jacques Pépin or Rachael Ray. Home cooking can be super simple; in fact, tossing together a salad from fresh greens and vegetables with a little protein counts as home cooking!

7. EAT A POUND OF PRODUCE A DAY

That's what the World Health Organization recommends, and it's what most of our health pros do. It's not difficult. A large apple, for instance, can easily be one-third of a pound. Tomato sauce counts. So do beans and lentils.

Studies show that people with a high intake of fruits and vegetables weigh less. They also get fiber, vitamins, minerals, and phytochemicals that protect against cancer and heart disease. "Eat the rainbow" has become a bit of a cliché, but it's the best way to think about how to eat a balanced diet. The compounds that give plants their pigments—green, purple, blue, red, orange, yellow—aren't just pretty. They're powerful antioxidants, and you want to eat a variety of them. Even white vegetables are good for you: Every ounce of them you eat each day reduces your stroke risk by 9 percent.

8. HAVE ONE MEATLESS DAY A WEEK

Meatless Mondays, semi-vegetarian, vegivore, vegan until 6 o'clock, flexitarian—these are just some of the words used to describe a way of eating that emphasizes plant foods but doesn't totally eschew dairy, meat, poultry, or fish. Maybe the best way to think about it is to consider yourself a vegetarian most of the time. In fact, one survey found that two out of three people who describe themselves as vegetarians actually eat this way. Most of the people in the Mediterranean (Italy, Greece, and Spain) follow this kind of diet, and study after study has shown that they have lower risks of chronic diseases. For instance, researchers at Loma Linda University School of Public Health in California found that the occurrence of diabetes in semi-vegetarians was about half that of people who ate a typical nonvegetarian diet. Harvard researchers found that limiting red meat intake to no more than $10\frac{1}{2}$ ounces a week could prevent 1 in 10 early deaths in men and 1 in 13 early deaths in women. And cutting out one serving of red meat per day lowered the risk of premature death by 7 to 19 percent, depending on whether the meat being eliminated was a burger or a roast or processed red meat. Another study showed that semi-vegetarians live an average of 3.6 years longer.

9. DESUGAR YOUR DIET

Evidence that added sugar plays a role not just in weight gain but also in heart disease, diabetes, cancer—and even wrinkles!—is steadily mounting. The average person eats 22 teaspoons, or 88 grams, of sugar a day. (Each teaspoon weighs 4 grams.) That's 352 calories' worth. The American Heart Association recommends a maximum daily intake of just 5 teaspoons for women and 6 teaspoons for men, which means that if you have one soda, you've already exceeded your limit. Our meals use only natural sugar (and some use maple syrup as a sugar replacer) from real whole fruits so you're not introducing extra sugar into your system.

Most of the sugar people eat isn't added to food by the teaspoon, though—it's in processed and packaged products. And separating added sugar from naturally occurring sugar in fruits, some veg-etables, dairy products, and whole grains isn't easy. The amount of sugar listed on food labels is the combination of both natural and added sugars in one serving of the food. Sugar has many names—high-fructose corn syrup, glucose, sucrose, honey, maple syrup, barley malt, beet sugar, cane juice, and cane sugar, to name a few—so reading the ingredients list can help. The best way to keep your added sugar intake low is to eat real foods.

10. SEPARATE YOUR MOOD FROM YOUR FOOD

Stress can ruin the best-laid diet plans. According to a survey by the American Psychological Association, 40 percent of respondents reported emotional eating—that is, eating for reasons other than hunger, such as feeling pressured, anxious, sad, or bored. (Interestingly, studies have found that being happy also causes people to eat more.) Stress appears to change the brain's response to food, making appetizing food more enticing—and it affects where your body stores fat. When your stress hormones are high, you tend to have more abdominal fat, which is linked to an increased risk of heart disease and diabetes. The solution is three pronged. First, eat mindfully (see rule 5). Second, find an outlet for your stress. In a University of California, San Francisco, study, mindful eating and meditation helped women feel less stressed and reduced stress hormones. The women in the study lost belly fat, even though they did not change what they ate. Exercise is also a terrific stress reliever.

Finally, learn to distinguish true hunger from head hunger—the desire to eat because you think you deserve it, because it will make you feel better, or just because the food looks good. How can you do this? Tune in to your body.

After you eat a meal, focus for a few minutes on your belly. You should feel satisfied but not stuffed, as though you could eat a few more bites, but you don't need to. (Don't check in too soon, though. Your brain needs 20 minutes to register that your stomach is full.) Once you become familiar with that feeling, ask yourself, "Am I hungry?" every time you want to eat. If the answer is yes, eat. If the answer is no, ask yourself what else is going on. Take 10 minutes to think about it—whatever you are craving will still be there—and then decide. Take a walk, read a book, call a friend—do anything you enjoy that will take your mind off of food. If that doesn't work, have a small portion of the food you want. That's often enough to make you feel satisfied. Whatever you do, though, don't beat yourself up. Even the best eaters give in to head hunger sometimes.

11. MOVE EVERY DAY

Okay, this isn't a diet tip, exactly, but exercise and diet are so closely linked that the connection can't be ignored. You don't need to do formal "exercise" every day, but whether it's climbing the stairs or walking the dog, just move your body. Being physically active often leads you to eat better. Some of that may just be a natural side effect of wanting to be healthy, but some researchers believe that exercise actually changes your brain so you are better able to resist temptation or so that the hormones that control your appetite are more balanced. People who get $2\frac{1}{2}$ hours of moderate activity a week have lower levels of inflammatory markers in their bloodstreams. And people who exercise are more sensitive to insulin (which lowers your risk for diabetes) and are less likely to develop dementia later in life. Exercise helps you sleep better, too, and people who get enough high-quality sleep are more likely to be slim.

The World's Best Foods

omen's Health is always on a mission to find the best, healthiest choices. We're your biggest cheerleader when it comes to your health. So when we decided to do a soups and smoothies book, we wanted only the healthiest ingredients to go into the recipes. You probably know that fresh fruits and vegetables and other "superfoods" are good for you, but do you know why? The healthiest foods contain essential vitamins and nutrients to give you glowing skin and shining hair, but they also protect the interior of our bodies from damaging free radicals. We figured you might not have time to do all the research, so we gathered the facts on the top healthiest foods and why you should be eating more of them.

APPLES

It's time to increase your apple IQ! Not only are apples among the most portable, inexpensive, and truly varied fruits (with 7,500 different kinds, there's an apple for every taste preference, from sweet to tart), they're also true health powerhouses. Their fiber content makes apples super satisfying. In one study, people who crunched on one 15 minutes before a meal ate 15 percent fewer calories at the meal. That translated to a 60-calorie deficit, once you factor in the calories in the apple. That may not sound like a lot, but if you did it once a day, you'd lose 6 pounds over the course of a year almost effortlessly.

About one-third of the fiber in apples is soluble, which is the type that helps to lower cholesterol. You need 3 to 5 grams of soluble fiber a day to get that effect; a medium apple has 2 grams. And apples keep your cardiovascular system ticking along in another way, too: They're rich in the antioxidant flavonoid quercetin and polyphenol compounds that have anti-inflammatory properties. A Dutch study found that having one medium apple a day can reduce your stroke risk by about 43 percent.

Apples looking a little better to you now?

ASPARAGUS

The next time you're serving veggies and dip, consider swapping out the celery sticks for asparagus spears. When it comes to nutrient density, this elegant vegetable is hard to beat. For a measly 28 calories, seven large spears provide 72 percent of your daily vitamin K—a nutrient required for blood clotting and bone health. You also get 3 grams of fiber, 20 percent of your daily vitamin A in the form of cancer-fighting carotenoids, 18 percent of your folate, 17 percent of your iron, and some vitamin B_6 and vitamin E.

And that's not all! Asparagus is a

good source of three compounds that are hard to find in many foods: inulin, glutathione, and saponins. Inulin is a type of fiber that has prebiotic properties. That means it serves as fuel for the healthy bacteria in your intestinal system, a characteristic that is probably responsible for asparagus's reputation as a folk remedy for digestive woes. Asparagus is considered a leading anti-inflammatory food in part due to its high concentration of glutathione, which some scientists consider to be the most powerful antioxidant. This compound strengthens your immune system's infection-fighting capabilities and also helps correct the cell damage that is often a first step in the development of cancer. Saponins are phytochemicals that may help lower cholesterol and reduce cancer risk.

While there are no studies to prove it, asparagus is said to have a diuretic effect and may help ease bloating. Those properties, combined with its high-fiber and low-calorie count, mean that asparagus is a good food to have in your diet if you're trying to lose weight. Some people also claim that asparagus alleviates hangovers. One small study found that asparagus extract enhanced the liver's ability to process alcohol and protected liver cells from the damage that alcohol can cause—but that was in test tubes. So go ahead and stick an asparagus spear in your Bloody Mary, if you like. Just don't expect it to protect you from a pounding head if you indulge in one too many.

AVOCADOS

Protect against:
Cancer, diabetes, heart disease, macular degeneration, and obesity

Key nutrients:
Beta-carotene, fiber, folate, lutein, monounsaturated fat, phytosterols, potassium, and zeaxanthin

Ever notice that when you have guacamole as an appetizer you barely have room for your tacos? That's because avocados are packed with a potent combination of fiber and healthy fats—there are 8 grams and 18 grams, respectively, in $\frac{1}{2}$ cup of guac! Including the creamy green fruit (yes, avocados are a fruit) with your meal can keep you feeling full. A study at Loma Linda University in California showed that people who had half an avocado produced more leptin—the fullness hormone—for up to 3 hours after they ate.

Two-thirds of the fat in avocados is monounsaturated, which helps lower insulin levels and facilitate weight loss. What's more, a mono-rich diet helps you lose belly fat specifically.

Monounsaturated fats provide a variety of other health benefits: They reduce inflammation, cholesterol, triglycerides, and blood sugar, and they ward off age-related memory decline. Monos even help keep skin plump and smooth by replenishing the protective layer of moisture-trapping fatty acids that surrounds skin cells.

Avocados are also the richest fruit source of phytosterols, compounds that alter the way your body processes cholesterol and may help lower LDL (or "bad") cholesterol levels. And avocados are packed with the B vitamin folate, which is important for heart health and for protecting against birth defects, as well as carotenoids such as beta-carotene, lutein, and zeaxanthin. These antioxidants help promote eye health and protect against cancer and heart disease. What's more, avocados help you absorb more of these antioxidants from any other foods you eat at the same time. In a study from Ohio State University, researchers served men and women lettuce, carrot, and spinach salads. When the salad contained avocado, the participants absorbed 8.3 times the alpha-carotene, 13.6 times the beta-carotene, and 4.3 times the lutein they did when they ate an avocado-free salad.

With so many benefits, there has to be a catch, right? Well yes, but it's a small one: The high fat content of avocados means they're also high in calories compared with other fruits and vegetables. Just one half of a medium-size avocado has 114 calories. So watch your portion sizes and have your guac with crudites instead of chips.

BEANS

Protect against:
  Diabetes, heart disease, and obesity

Key nutrients:
  Antioxidants, folate, potassium, protein, and soluble fiber

We all know the old adage about beans, but they are indeed good for your heart—and the rest of your body, too. They're the chameleons of the food world, able to play a variety of nutritional roles. Beans can count as a protein, a "good" carb, and even a vegetable serving.

One of their most powerful properties is soluble fiber. Beans contain more of this compound than almost any other food. Soluble fiber absorbs water in your digestive tract, which means it leaves your stomach slowly, having a beneficial effect on your weight (because you feel fuller longer) and your blood sugar levels. In a report from the National Health and Nutrition Examination survey, scientists found that people who ate beans were 23 percent less likely to have large waists than those who never ate beans. And researchers from the University of Toronto found that people with type 2 diabetes who ate mostly low-glycemic-index foods such as nuts and beans improved their blood sugar levels and were at lower risk for heart disease than people who ate mostly whole grain breads, cereals, and brown rice.

Soluble fiber also interferes with the absorption of dietary cholesterol, so it can lower your blood cholesterol levels. Researchers at Arizona State University Polytechnic in Mesa found that adding $1/2$ cup of beans to soup reduces cholesterol levels by up to 8 percent.

Black beans, red kidney beans, and other dark-colored beans are as high or higher in antioxidants as colorful fruits and vegetables. But that doesn't mean that paler beans have no value. For instance, white beans give you 100 milligrams of calcium per $1/2$ cup—a respectable amount! And lentils are one of the best sources of the B vitamin folate, which is so important in lowering the risk of birth defects and also plays a role in heart and brain health.

The rest of that childhood chant—the line that rhymes with *heart*—is, unfortunately, also true. Beans contain complex sugars called oligosaccharides that can't be digested. They are fermented by the good bacteria in your gut, producing gas and bloating. But you can both reduce beans' oligosaccharides and make your body more resistant to them. Soaking beans overnight and then cooking them in fresh water or rinsing canned beans can help remove the sugars. (Rinsing canned beans also removes about 40 percent of their sodium, so it's a good idea whether you suffer from bean-related bloat or not.) Drink lots of water when you eat beans (or any other high-fiber food), and start with small portions so your digestive system adjusts. That way, you get the health benefits without the unpleasant consequences.

BERERIES

Protect against:
Cancer, diabetes, heart disease, memory loss, and obesity

Key nutrients:
Anthocyanins, antioxidants, fiber, and vitamin C

It's amazing what eating just a handful of berries can do for your health. In a study involving 200,000 men and women, those who ate 1 cup of blueberries a week had a 23 percent lower risk of developing diabetes. Having $\frac{1}{2}$ cup of blueberries or 1 cup of strawberries a week protected the brains of elderly women (with an average age of 74) from age-related memory decline. Harvard researchers estimated that the berry eaters delayed their cognitive decline by as much as $2\frac{1}{2}$ years.

The "magic" ingredients in berries responsible for these benefits appear to be anthocyanins—red and blue pigments that are powerful antioxidants. These compounds have also been linked to a lower risk of a variety of cancers. On top of that, each berry type comes with its own nutritional bonus: Blueberries have the highest concentration of anthocyanins. Raspberries have the most fiber—at 8 grams per cup, ounce for ounce more than any other fruit. One cup of strawberries has more vitamin C than you need in a day. Cranberries have five times the antioxidant power of broccoli, plus they're a natural probiotic, which means they'll enhance good bacteria levels and protect you from foodborne illnesses. Blackberries help lower cholesterol and blood pressure, and they can play a key role in keeping diabetes, heart disease, and cancer at bay. And berries have some of the lowest calorie counts of all fruits, ranging from 53 per cup for strawberries to 84 per cup for blueberries.

Although berries are delicate and their season is short, you can freeze fresh berries for up to a year, or you can buy packaged frozen ones. Just be sure to check the labels as some brands come loaded with sugar. Cranberries in their natural state are so tart that cranberry

products are often terribly oversweet-
ened. You're much better off buying

fresh cranberries to make your soup
or smoothie.

BROCCOLI

Protects against:
Cancer and heart disease

Key nutrients:
Fiber, folate, sulforaphane, and
vitamin C

Maligned by a president and millions of
picky eaters, broccoli has a reputation
for being a bitter-tasting vegetable with
an unpleasant odor. But that's not broccoli's fault—blame the chef! Too often
broccoli is overcooked, which turns it an
unappetizing, drab green, makes it mushy,
and concentrates the sulfur compounds
that are responsible for some of its strong
flavor. If you've been a broccoli-hater, you
owe it to your health to give it another
try. Along with other members of the
cruciferous family, like cabbage, cauliflower, Brussels sprouts, broccoli rabe,
bok choy, and turnips, broccoli is a true
nutrition all-star.

Let's start with the basics: A cup of
broccoli gives you a hefty dose of calcium, manganese, potassium, phosphorus, magnesium, iron, fiber, folate, and
vitamins C and K. It also has 3 grams of

protein. Broccoli's cancer-fighting compounds include carotenoids and especially sulforaphane. Japanese
researchers found that women with
breast cancer who ate a lot of broccoli
and other cruciferous vegetables cut
their risk of a recurrence by 35 percent
and their chances of dying from the disease by 62 percent in a 3-year period.
Other studies have shown that men at
risk for prostate cancer who ate about a
pound of broccoli a week experienced
more gene changes linked to a reduced
chance of developing cancer, and that
eating cruciferous vegetables even cut
the odds of lung cancer in smokers by
20 to 55 percent. (But don't use that as
an excuse to smoke!)

The saddest thing about overcooking
broccoli is that it destroys many of the
nutrients. To get the benefits of broccoli
and learn to love it, blanch it in boiling
water for a few minutes, or steam it
until it turns bright green. That's when
you know it's tender enough to eat but
still crunchy enough to enjoy. Serving

broccoli with whole grains or nuts helps to soften the bitterness, as does pairing it with sweeter vegetables like red peppers, carrots, or caramelized onions.

Stir-frying broccoli with garlic does the trick, too. If all else fails, try broccolini, which has a similar nutritional profile but a milder, peppery flavor.

COFFEE

Protects against:
Cancer, diabetes, Parkinson's disease, and stroke

Key nutrients:
Boron, caffeine, chromium, and polyphenols

Whether we get it from a specialty shop, a good old-fashioned diner, or a pot in the kitchen, Americans love coffee. We drink an average of 3 cups per person each day. Although we savor that warm comfort, soothing aroma, and caffeine hit, most of us at one time or another have wondered: How bad is this for me? Relax. Coffee, in fact, has many perks.

Swedish researchers found that women who drink 5 cups a day are 57 percent less likely to get an aggressive form of breast cancer than those who don't drink coffee. And according to another study, just 1 cup a day protects against liver cancer.

But the powers of this magical brew don't stop there. Drinking more than

1 daily cup of coffee is associated with a 22 to 25 percent lower risk of stroke, according to a study in the journal *Stroke*. Harvard researchers found that coffee lowers your odds of developing type 2 diabetes by 29 to 54 percent. And having 1 to 3 cups a day cuts your risk of Parkinson's disease, enhances short-term memory, and helps prevent dementia.

Most of the disease-fighting benefits of coffee don't come courtesy of caffeine, but are due to its polyphenol antioxidants. Coffee is right up there with fruit as a source of these compounds, and because of our high intake, it's the number one source of antioxidants in the American diet.

That doesn't mean, though, that caffeine has no value. While consuming too much can leave you jittery and can interfere with sleep, it does keep you alert. It also improves your endurance. In one study, recreational runners improved their 5K times by 1 percent after drinking a cup of high-test coffee. A study in the journal *Physiology and Behavior* showed that caffeine boosts metabolism by about 16 percent. And people who drank caffeinated coffee had a lower risk of basal cell carcinoma, the most common type of skin cancer, according to a study in *Cancer Research*. (Decaf was not protective.) A word to the wise: Take your java black or with a little milk or cream. Gourmet coffee drinks can contain more calories and sugar than a can of soda.

DARK CHOCOLATE

Protects against:
Depression, diabetes, heart disease, and obesity

Key nutrients:
Flavonoids

Turns out, you can have your chocolate and eat it, too! In recent years, scientific findings have revealed that this guilty pleasure is actually a bona fide health food. Cocoa and dark chocolate that contain at least 70 percent cacao are rich in antioxidant flavonoids and, in fact, have among the highest antioxidant concentrations of any foods. These antioxidants can provide a multitude of benefits, including keeping your arteries flexible and improving your circulation. People who eat chocolate may be 37 percent less likely to develop heart disease and 29 percent less likely to have a stroke than those who don't, according to a British study. And there's evidence that chocolate can be cardioprotective even if you already have heart disease. A Swedish study published in the *Journal of Internal Medicine* shows that heart attack survivors who snacked on chocolate just twice a week were 70 percent less likely to die from cardiac problems. More flexible arteries benefit your brain, too. After drinking a cup of hot cocoa, people in one study were able to count backward more quickly and accurately than they did when they did not drink cocoa, and they were less likely to feel tired or mentally drained.

Chocolate eaters are also happier, calmer people because daily hits of the treat reduce levels of stress hormones, according to a study in the *Journal of Proteome Research*. Other studies show that the phenethylamine chocolate contains triggers the production of endorphins and results in a feeling of well-being that's similar to falling in love. In one study, couples were connected to brain and heart monitors, given chocolate, and then told to kiss. Both the chocolate and the kissing alone made hearts pound and brains buzz, but the addition of chocolate doubled excitation rates in the brain's pleasure center during the kiss, especially in women.

Paradoxically, giving in to chocolate cravings can help you drop pounds. In one study, people who were offered pizza $2\frac{1}{2}$ hours after eating dark chocolate ate 15 percent fewer calories than they did when they had milk chocolate. And researchers at the University of California, San Diego, conducted a study that made them suspect that the calories in chocolate are metabolized in such a way that they don't lead to weight gain. Dark chocolate lovers were thinner than those who ate very little of the treat, even though they didn't consume fewer calories overall or exercise more. Still, you want to keep your chocolate fix healthy, so stick to small servings and pair it with other antioxidant-rich foods, like fruit or nuts.

DARK LEAFY GREENS

Protect against:
Cancer, diabetes, macular degeneration, and obesity

Key nutrients:
Calcium, carotenoids, fiber, folate, iron, vitamin C, and vitamin K

Nutritionists like to talk about "nutrient density": the amount of nutrients you get from a food relative to its calorie count. From mild-tasting romaine lettuce and spinach, to peppery arugula and mesclun, to pleasantly bitter escarole, kale, Swiss chard, and collards, calorie for calorie, dark leafy greens are among the most nutritious foods on the planet. For instance, 1 cup of cooked kale provides 1,327 percent of your daily vitamin K, 354 percent of your vitamin A (in the form of antioxidant carotenoids), 89 percent of your vitamin C, 9 percent of your calcium, 8 percent of your iron and potassium, 6 percent of your magnesium, 4 percent of your folate and vitamin E, and 3 grams of fiber. It also contains sulforaphane—a cancer-fighting compound found in cruciferous vegetables.

All that for just 36 calories. To one degree or another, all leafy greens (even iceberg lettuce) contain the same nutrients. But the darker the green, the more nutritious it is. Iceberg lovers, try romaine: It has the same refreshing crunch, but 9 times the carotenoids, 7.5 times the vitamin C, 4 times the folate, and 3.6 times the vitamin K.

Their carotenoid content makes dark leafy greens potent cancer fighters as well as vision protectors. Lutein, a carotenoid abundant in greens, has been linked to a lower risk of macular degeneration (the leading cause of blindness) and cataracts. Vitamin K is a powerful anti-inflammatory, and some studies suggest that it helps protect against arthritis. It's also an important component of bone health.

The strong flavors of some of the deepest-hued greens make people shy away from them, but there are a few things you can do to make them more palatable. Blanch sturdy greens like kale and collards in boiling water until the color turns vibrant, about 2 to 3 minutes. Then sauté the greens with garlic in a flavorful olive oil. For salads, you can combine milder-tasting greens with peppery ones.

It's worth the effort to learn to love greens. Having just one serving a day (1 cup of raw greens or $1/2$ cup of cooked) cuts your heart attack risk by about 23 percent, according to a report from the Harvard Nurses' Health Study. More is better: Italian researchers found that women who eat 2 ounces of greens a day (about $1^1/_2$ cups of raw spinach or 1 cup of chopped raw kale) lowered their odds of developing heart disease by about 46 percent. And a study from the University of Leicester found a strong connection between dark leafy greens and a reduced risk of type 2 diabetes. Those who ate at least $1^1/_2$ servings a day were 14 percent less likely to develop the disease, something the researchers attribute to the high magnesium levels in greens. Need a little extra incentive? Researchers at the University of Munich found that people scored about 20 percent higher on a creativity test when they got a glimpse of the color green beforehand. They believe our brains associate the color with nature, which leads us to think about growth and development. So the next time you're feeling uninspired, toss yourself a dark green salad!

MANGOES

Protect against:
Diabetes, digestive problems, heart disease, and obesity

Key nutrients:
Carotenoids, fiber, vitamin C, and vitamin E

The next time someone complains that "healthy foods are bland and boring," hand her a mango and watch what happens. Sweet, juicy, tropical mangoes taste luscious and decadent but are some of the healthiest fruits around. In one study, people who ate 1¼ cups of mango daily for a month experienced a 37 percent drop in triglyceride levels, which helps cut heart disease risk. Another heart-healthy perk of mangoes is that they contain the antioxidant vitamin E. Mangoes' antioxidant carotenoids not only make them a good source of vitamin A, supplying 36 percent of your daily needs in just 1 cup, but they also help protect against cancer.

Mangoes make a flavorful side dish or topping for poultry, pork, or fish, and they contain enzymes that help your body break down the protein in these foods. One cup also supplies 10 percent of your fiber needs. Both properties ease digestion.

Although the research is preliminary, mangoes may enhance fat burning. Researchers at Oklahoma State University in Stillwater found that mice that were fed mangoes as part of their diets for 2 months weighed the same as mice that were not, but they had less body fat and low blood glucose levels. When glucose is low, the body produces less insulin, a hormone that can boost fat storage. Low glucose also means a lower risk of diabetes. How's that for some sweet news?

NUTS AND NUT BUTTERS

Protect against:
Alzheimer's disease, heart disease, and obesity

Key nutrients:
Calcium, healthy fats, magnesium, protein, and vitamin E

When it comes to the nutritional benefits of nuts, the list just keeps growing. In addition to helping your heart, they also boost your brainpower. A study published in the journal *Neurology* showed that elderly people who ate diets rich in vitamin E and omega-3 fatty acids were less likely to have brain shrinkage and more likely to perform well on cognitive tests than those who didn't. And those almonds you've been eating? You can subtract about 30 percent from their calorie count, because USDA scientists found that they have only 129 calories per ounce, not 170. Another study by the same group showed pistachios to be lower in calories as well. This trend likely applies to all nuts.

But even before this research was released, nuts were known to be big players in weight control, thanks to the healthy fats, protein, and fiber they contain all in one little package. In a Harvard University study, people who had walnuts at breakfast stayed full all morning and ate fewer calories at lunch. And nuts can rev your metabolism. Researchers from Georgia Southern University in Statesboro found that having a high-protein, high-fat snack increases calorie burn for more than 3 hours afterward!

Still, it's easy to go overboard when eating nuts. Measure out a 1-ounce portion—about $^1/_4$ cup of nuts. If one handful just leads to another, try buying unshelled nuts and cracking them yourself. According to a study published in *Appetite,* noshing on pistachios you have to shell yourself can help decrease the number of calories you take in by more than 40 percent. This is probably because shelling the nuts makes you more mindful of how many you're eating and slows you down, giving your brain time to register that your appetite is being satisfied.

Each nut has its own unique nutritional benefit. Almonds are a good source of calcium, walnuts are packed with cardioprotective omega-3s, and just one Brazil nut more than satisfies your daily requirement of selenium, a mineral that may help protect against cancer. All nuts have antioxidants, but pecans have the most. As is true for vegetables and fruit, eating a variety of nuts is better than eating just one type. You might try keeping a container of mixed nuts at your desk or in your pantry for an easy snack. Just be sure to keep your serving size in check because nuts are not low in calories.

OATS

Whether you're a traditionalist who likes hearty steel-cut oats or someone who prefers the quickness of a bowl of oat-Os cereal, you'll be happy to know that either form of this whole grain serves up valuable nutrients.

Oats are one of the best sources of beta-glucan, a soluble fiber that lowers cholesterol levels. Soluble fiber binds to the cholesterol-based acids in your digestive tract; that means that when the fiber leaves your body, it takes the cholesterol with it. In turn, your liver has to make more of those acids, so it snags cholesterol from your bloodstream, lowering your blood levels of that substance.

In an 8-week University of Connecticut study, men with high LDL cholesterol who got a daily dose of soluble fiber from oats experienced a more than 20 percent drop in cholesterol levels. Other studies show that you need about 3 to 5 grams of soluble fiber a day—1½ cups of cooked oatmeal have 3 grams—to reap this ben-

efit. This protein-rich grain is also high in a type of antioxidant called avenanthramides, which protect LDL cholesterol from oxidation (the first step in the buildup of the arterial plaque that can raise heart attack risk).

The fiber in oats means they're digested slowly, so they keep you full. Oatmeal ranked third in a satiety index developed by Australian researchers who compared 240-calorie portions of various foods. And when Harvard University researchers analyzed the diets of more than 27,000 men over the course of 8 years, they found that the men who added one serving of whole grain foods to their daily diets weighed 2.5 pounds less than the men who ate only foods made from refined grains.

Although instant oatmeal has the same amount of soluble fiber ounce for ounce as rolled or steel-cut oats, it is not as filling. That's because when the oats are sliced to cook quickly, their glycemic index—the rate at which they are digested and converted to glucose in the bloodstream—rises. Plus, flavored instant oatmeal is often a vehicle for sugar, with about 3 teaspoons of added sugar in each little packet. The truth is that you don't save all that much time with the instant stuff—rolled oats (also called old-fashioned oats) cook up in just 5 minutes and they, too, are perfectly microwaveable.

OLIVE OIL

Bone loss, cancer, heart disease, obesity, and stroke

Antioxidants, monounsaturated fat, and vitamin K

The centerpiece of Mediterranean cuisine, olive oil is at least partially responsible for the diet's health benefits—but only if you pick the right type. Any olive oil is an excellent source of monounsaturated fat, but getting one with lots of other beneficial compounds takes a little thought. To pick the healthiest oil, don't rely on labels, but trust your taste buds. True cold-pressed extra virgin olive oil (the kind to buy for both flavor and health) has a slightly bitter, peppery flavor. You should feel a little sting in the back of your throat or the urge to cough when you taste it straight; that's a sign that the oil is rich in anti-inflammatories, polyphenols, and antioxidants.

Olive oil is at its most therapeutic and flavorful when it is as fresh as possible.

Light, air, and time decrease the beneficial compounds in the oil, so skip the brands packaged in clear bottles, never buy an olive oil that doesn't have a "best by" stamp and a date a few months away, and don't be tempted by the deal on the 5-gallon can at the warehouse store. You should buy only as much as you will use in a few months. Real olive oil isn't cheap, but a high price is no guarantee of quality. Try to buy your olive oil at a store that will let you taste it beforehand (or return it if you don't like it), and remember that a little goes a long way.

Now that you know how to snag the good stuff, here's why olive oil should be a staple in your kitchen for both cooking and drizzling. For one thing, it will make your heart happy. Monounsaturated fats prevent the oxidation of LDL ("bad") cholesterol, a process that leads to clogged arteries. In one study, people who consumed the most olive oil had a 44 percent lower risk of dying from heart disease (and a 26 percent lower risk of dying from any cause) during the study period compared to those who ate the least olive oil. French researchers found that using extra virgin olive oil for both cooking and eating lowers stroke risk by 41 percent. While a group of Spanish scientists were studying the effect of the Mediterranean diet on heart disease, they discovered that elderly men who ate olive oil had a dramatic increase in blood markers that signal bone formation, while those who followed a Mediterranean-style diet with nuts and no oil or a low-fat diet did not.

Another reason to stock up on olive oil: The polyphenols and antioxidants it contains have antibacterial properties that kill the bacteria that cause ulcers. Those compounds also have been shown to protect against various cancers.

Finally, foods high in monounsaturated fat help you burn belly fat, and olive oil is no exception. It also appears to be more satisfying than other fats. Researchers at Pennsylvania State University in State College found that a lunch cooked in olive oil keeps you fuller longer than the exact same food cooked in corn oil. Food specialists at the University of Illinois at Urbana-Champaign gave 341 Italian restaurant patrons equal amounts of bread and either olive oil or butter. The olive oil group ate 26 percent more fat on each slice of bread, but the butter eaters ate more bread and therefore consumed about 17 percent more calories.

The message here, though, isn't that you should pour olive oil all over everything. At 120 per tablespoon, the calories in olive oil add up quickly, so be sure to measure.

QUINOA

Protects against:
Cancer, diabetes, heart disease, and obesity

Key nutrients
Antioxidants, fiber, folate, iron, magnesium, phosphorus, and protein

With gluten-free diets gaining popularity, you may have noticed a new addition to the grain aisle at your local supermarket: quinoa (pronounced KEEN-wah). But quinoa really isn't new at all; in fact, it was a staple food for Inca warriors, who prized the grain for its energy-giving powers.

Quinoa is not actually a grain, although it certainly cooks up like one. It's a seed that's botanically related to beets and Swiss chard, and it has some unique nutritional properties among "grains." It's higher in protein, for one thing, and that protein is complete, meaning it has all eight essential amino acids, just like eggs and meat do. All whole grains contain antioxidants, but quinoa is particularly packed with quercetin and kaempferol, anti-inflammatory compounds linked to a lower risk of cancer and heart disease. Quercetin is also a natural antihistamine.

Like whole grains, quinoa helps to stabilize blood sugar because it has a low glycemic index and it's high in fiber. That makes it valuable for weight control and diabetes prevention.

There are culinary advantages as well. Quinoa is nuttier and more flavorful than brown rice, and it cooks in just 15 to 20 minutes. Unlike grains, which are soft and chewy, quinoa is both soft and crunchy. When you cook it, the germ of the seed twists out and forms a crunchy "tail." It tastes good hot or cold, can be used in sweet or savory dishes, and comes in three colors: ivory, red, and black. Take any rice or pasta recipe and sub in quinoa. You won't be sorry!

TEA

Protects against:
Arthritis, bone loss, cancer, diabetes, heart disease, obesity, stroke, and viral infections

Key nutrients:
Caffeine and catechins

For a beverage with such a quiet, meditative, and somewhat fussy reputation, tea certainly packs a powerful health punch. The different varieties of tea—white, green, oolong, and black—all contain antioxidant polyphenols called catechins. The most powerful of these is EGCG, found in highest concentration in green tea. Studies have linked regular consumption of green tea to a lower risk of colon, breast, gastric, lung, and prostate cancers. Researchers at the University of Parma in Italy studied 32 men with a type of precancerous prostate change that develops into cancer within 1 year of diagnosis about 30 percent of the time. The men took 200 milligrams of green tea catechins (the amount in about 1 cup of tea) three times a day for a year, and only one developed prostate cancer. White tea also has disease-fighting properties. A study at Kingston University in London tested 21 plant and herb extracts and found white tea to be the most effective at reducing inflammation, thereby lowering your odds of rheumatoid arthritis, some cancers, and wrinkles.

EGCG is also a metabolism booster. Researchers at the USDA found that people burned an extra 67 calories a day when they drank oolong tea instead of the same amount of caffeinated water. They believe that something in the tea other than caffeine, most likely the catechins, encourages the body to burn fat for energy first (rather than carbohydrates). Fat oxidation was 12 percent higher when the study volunteers were drinking tea. In a small Japanese study, men burned 17 percent more fat during a 30-minute workout when they drank green tea beforehand.

But everyday black tea is no health slouch, either. People who drink a cup of it after eating high-carb foods decrease their blood sugar levels by 10 percent for 2½ hours, according to a study published in the *Journal of the American College of Nutrition*. Black tea also reduces blood pressure and helps you combat LDL ("bad") cholesterol, lowering it by up to 10 percent in only 3 weeks.

Your immune system gets a helping hand from tea, too. Drinking a cup zaps viruses, such as the kinds that cause colds and flu, within 10 minutes, scientists at Pace University in New York City found. Have a sinus infection? Researchers at Alexandria University in Egypt found that green tea enhances the action of antibiotics, in some cases by threefold. Even allergy sufferers can get a break: EGCG may block the allergenic response some people have to pollen, pet dander, and dust.

And if all of that's not enough, here's the kicker: Tea can help slow the bone loss that comes with age. An Australian study found that tea-drinking women between the ages of 70 and 85 had greater bone density than women of the same age who did not drink tea.

Herbal tea doesn't have the same antioxidants that regular tea does, but it does have its own health benefits. For example, chamomile and peppermint can soothe upset stomachs, passionflower helps you sleep, rosemary wards off stress-induced headaches, and thyme alleviates coughing and sinus pressure.

Iced tea is just as powerful as hot tea, if you make it yourself; the bottled stuff varies widely in antioxidant content. And scientists can't seem to agree on the effect milk has on tea's antioxidants. Some studies show that milk protein binds the beneficial compounds, yet others show it doesn't make a difference. Until the jury comes in, drink at least a few of your cups straight up.

YOGURT

Protects against:

Digestive problems, heart disease, high blood pressure, obesity, and osteoporosis

Key nutrients:

Calcium, potassium, probiotics, protein, and vitamin B_{12}

You probably think of yogurt as a great source of calcium, and you wouldn't be wrong. (There's only one other food that is a better natural source of this mineral than yogurt, and that's ricotta cheese.) A 6-ounce container of nonfat plain yogurt has about 300 milligrams, or 30 percent of what you need each day.

But yogurt supplies so much more. First there's the protein, a hefty 8 grams, surpassing the amount in a large egg or $1/2$ cup of kidney beans. Nonfat Greek yogurt has more protein (18 grams) than regular yogurt, but also less calcium (200 milligrams). Next up is potassium— 468 milligrams in 6 ounces, close to the amount in a large banana. Calcium and potassium work together to lower blood pressure. One study found that two servings of low-fat dairy a day cut the odds of developing hypertension by 54 percent.

Turning milk into yogurt requires the addition of healthy bacteria. Two strains—*Lactobacillus bulgaricus* and *Streptococcus thermophilus*—are used for this purpose. Many also contain *L. acidophilus*, which is a probiotic, a bacteria that takes up residence in your digestive tract and helps keep you healthy in several ways. (Many yogurt manufacturers add other probiotic strains to their products.) Probiotics have been shown to boost the immune system. In one study, elderly people who ate about 3 ounces of yogurt a day were 2.6 times less likely to catch colds than those who didn't eat yogurt. Antibiotics decrease the number of healthy bacteria in your gut, which can lead to diarrhea. Eating yogurt helps you repopulate the good bacteria and reduces your odds of experiencing this unpleasant side effect by about 60 percent. Probiotics are also being studied for their role in heart disease prevention and weight control.

The calcium and protein combo in yogurt has been shown to make dropping pounds easier. A study from the Harvard School of Public Health that looked at the diet habits of more than 120,000 people for two decades found that consumption of nuts and yogurt was most closely correlated with weight loss. And yogurt seems particularly effective in burning belly fat. University of Tennessee, Knoxville, researchers found that women who lost weight eating yogurt had 81 percent less fat around their waists than those who didn't eat yogurt.

All of these weight-loss benefits come from eating plain yogurt. The sugar-filled stuff is candy in disguise, in many instances. Some of the sugar in fruit yogurts comes from lactose in the milk itself (anything with -ose at the end is a sugar) or from the fruit. Even a plain, unsweetened, low-fat yogurt has 12 grams of sugar in a 6-ounce container. These natural sugars aren't a problem, but fruit and flavored yogurts often contain added sugar in the form of sucrose or high-fructose corn syrup. Different brands add different amounts, and both natural and added sugars are lumped together on food labels. Your very best defense is to buy plain yogurt and add your own fruit, or even a little honey, if you like. That way, you control how much sugar you eat. Your second-best option is to read labels carefully and pick a flavored yogurt with as close to 12 grams of sugar as possible. If you don't mind sugar substitutes, yogurts made with them will have the same amount of sugar as an equal portion of plain yogurt.

INDEX

Underscored page references indicate boxed text and tips. **Boldfaced** page references indicate photographs.